Christie Musso

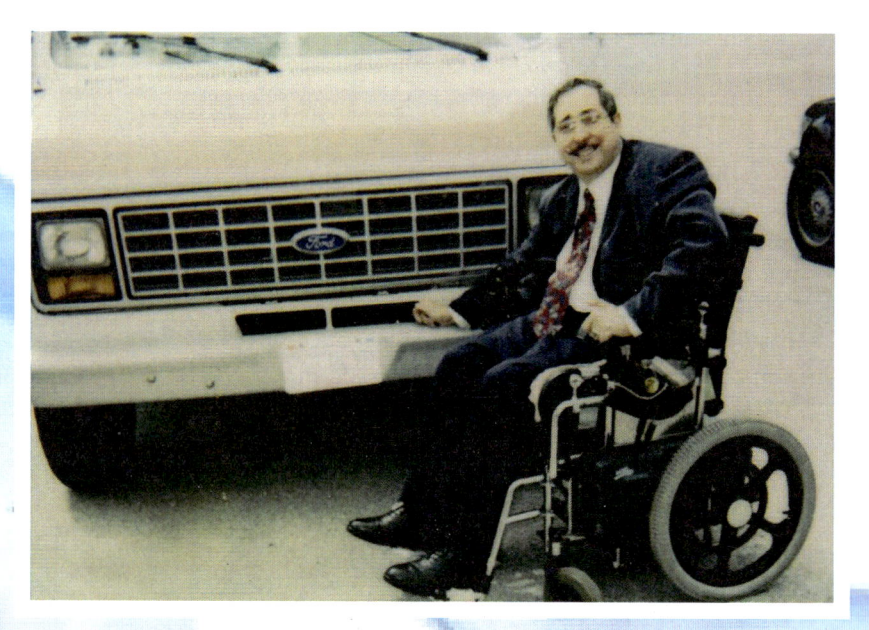

My Dad

My Mom

The Girls Home Indianapolis Indiana

The "hole" where we were kept in the basement

My best friend Beth

My Roommate at the girls home

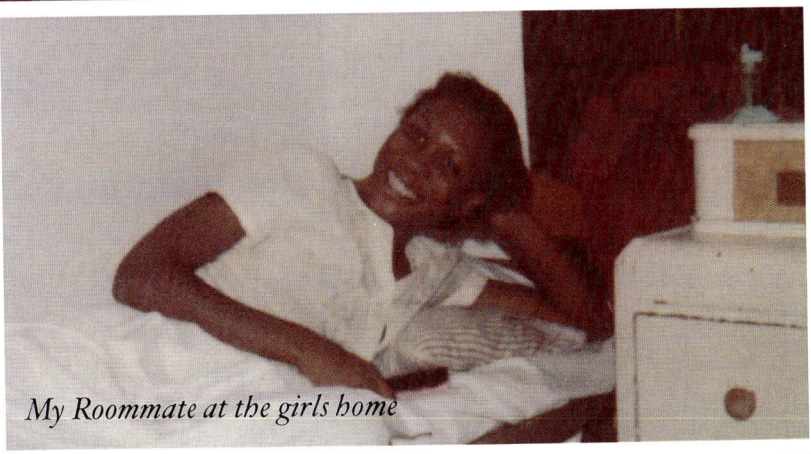

Christie Musso

My son Daniel who is a paramedic for Life Saver in Birmingham, Alabama

My daughter Katie who is a paramedic in Huntsville, Alabama

*Me and both my children
at my daughters college graduation*

My son Daniel and my grandson Aaron

My daughter Katie

Christie Musso

My sister Barbara McCoy

My best friend Linda Brewer

My walking examples of Jesus David and Missy Cooper

My best friend Missy Cooper

Pastor Matthew Roskam and family Chelsea Creek Community Church Birmingham Alabama

My sponsor Sue Rich

My circle of friends

My husband David on our wedding day

My husband David who committed Suicide

My husband David who committed Suicide

In Hope Knows Your Name, you will see your identity is not in your past or current situation, but in Christ.

Have you ever felt, or perhaps still deal with, feelings of inadequacy, self-esteem, fear, abandonment, rejection, or worthlessness? Do you have love or relationship issues or perhaps just feel a sense of plain hopelessness? Have you experienced a void in your life that you have chosen to fill in unhealthy ways, or have been unable to fill? If you can relate, or you know someone else who does, this book is for you.

The greatest gift we can give each other is to be honest about ourselves. That is exactly what you will find in my sharing of my heart's journey through the most intimate details of my life. I am a survivor of childhood physical, sexual and emotional abuse, and a survivor of a spouse who committed suicide in the federal courthouse. My brokenness is what brought me to my knees. However, it was God's grace, forgiveness, and unconditional love that brought me to the point of realizing---He is enough.

My story is truly one of learning how to weather life in the midst of the storm. In reading my book, you will see your identity is not in your past or current situation, but in Christ. You will know, beyond a shadow of a doubt that He is madly in love with you, you are completely forgiven, fully pleasing, and totally accepted, and complete in Him.

Romans 5:3 says you can rejoice in your sufferings, because suffering produces perseverance, perseverance produces character, and character produces hope. No matter where you find yourself in this thing we call life, as you will see by my story, Hope Knows Your Name.

HOPE
KNOWS YOUR NAME

HOPE
KNOWS YOUR NAME
CLINGING TO GOD'S GRACE IN LIFE'S STORMS

CHRISTIE MUSSO

TATE PUBLISHING
AND ENTERPRISES, LLC

Hope Knows Your Name
Copyright © 2014 by Christie Musso. All rights reserved.

No part of this publication may be reproduced, stored in a retrieval system or transmitted in any way by any means, electronic, mechanical, photocopy, recording or otherwise without the prior permission of the author except as provided by USA copyright law.

The opinions expressed by the author are not necessarily those of Tate Publishing, LLC.

Published by Tate Publishing & Enterprises, LLC
127 E. Trade Center Terrace | Mustang, Oklahoma 73064 USA
1.888.361.9473 | www.tatepublishing.com

Tate Publishing is committed to excellence in the publishing industry. The company reflects the philosophy established by the founders, based on Psalm 68:11,
"The Lord gave the word and great was the company of those who published it."

Book design copyright © 2014 by Tate Publishing, LLC. All rights reserved.
Cover design by Nikolai Purpura
Interior design by Jomel Pepito

Published in the United States of America

ISBN: 978-1-63063-258-8
1. Self-Help / Personal Growth / General
2. Religion / Christian Life / Personal Growth
14.10.20

Dedication

To my mom, Rosemarie

Not only are you my mom, but you are truly my hero and my best friend. It amazes me that with everything you had to overcome in your own life; that you can, and do, still live life with such passion. Thank you for showing me by example, that if I put my heart into something, and have the will to do the work that I can accomplish anything I set my mind to. You have an amazing drive for life, which you have also instilled in me. Thank you for believing in me and for continuously encouraging me to believe in myself. You have always encouraged me to pursue my dreams and continuously remind me that no matter what, not to ever stop believing in myself or in my dreams. And if I do fail, to pick myself up, brush myself off, and keep on going. I love you.

*To my children Daniel and Katie and
my precious grandson Aaron.*

There were very few things I did right in my life, but I know for certain that those few things were having the two of you. While growing up, you both have had to go through some pretty tough things that you should have never had to, nor did you deserve. It amazes me to see how the both of you walked through all that hardship, and came out better people which have made you the incredible adults you are today. You have shown first hand that suffering produces perseverance, perseverance produces character, and character produces hope. The both of you have an incredible drive for life even in the midst of all the adversity that you both were raised in. What you have accomplished is the ultimate of amazing. It did not surprise me at all to see the both of you become paramedics soaking your lives into helping others. That is just who you are and who you have become in spite of your own life struggles. Daniel, thank you for one of the many things you have done right, and that was giving me my precious grandson Aaron. You are such an amazing father and watching you love that little guy like you do, is just indescribable. Seeing you give him that unique gift of having a father who loves him, protects him, and gives him security, is just beyond any words I can say. I love that little guy more than you will ever know, just as I love the two of you more than you will ever know. Daniel, you went from becoming a firefighter, to the military, to becoming a paramedic and now a flight medic with Lifesaver, living your dream.

You just amaze me when the odds were against you; you grabbed life and took off with it. Katie-bug, I really let you down when I left your father and I know your life was very hard because of a lot of my choices. In spite of all that, you have a drive for life that is impeccable. You have worked so hard to make it on your own, never asking for anything. Working full time, you still chose to go on to college to become a paramedic and the night you graduated from college was my all-time high. I am so proud of you. You are still so young at age twenty three; I cannot wait to see what is ahead in your future, and to know I have the privilege of being your mom and watching it. You both have made me so proud and though not deserved, I am honored to be called your mom. Thank you both for loving me and supporting me like you do, even when I did not deserve it.

*To my sister Barbara and
my nephews Donnie and Jonathon.*

I am so blessed to call you all my family. Barbara I know you had a huge part in helping take care of me when I was young, which caused you to have to grow up very quickly. You have always done a great job as a big sister and I love you very much. Donnie and Jonathon, I love you two guys so much, although we all don't see each other as much as I would like. You both have a very special place in my heart and I thank you for loving me even through all my craziness. All three of you have done a great job at loving me well, even when I have not been so loveable.

In memory of my father Ross

Dad, although I am sharing my story which you were a huge part. I love you more than you will ever know, and I miss you. My only regret is that I had not forgiven you long before I did where we could have spent some good years together before you died. Even though you are gone, I have forgiven you, and I am by no means sharing my story, to shame you, but to let others see what I had to walk through, how God got me through it, and to show others whose parents were absent from their lives, that there is someone who can fill that void, and his name is Jesus. I find comfort in knowing that you are looking down on me and see that by sharing my story, about our true life situation with each other, that we are opening the door to helping millions because of what you and I walked through. Thank you daddy for having a huge part in me becoming the godly woman I have become today, knowing first hand that hope never dies.

In memory of my husband David, who committed suicide.

My prayer in writing this book is that it will give so much hope to so many others, that they never feel as if they have to do what you did. I hope that in reading my book others can come to the realization that no one, nor any situation, is hopeless. In this life, I will probably never fully understand what you did, or why you did it. But the day I married you was one of the happiest days of my life, and the day you took yours was by far my worse. This incident put me in one of the darkest places I have ever been, but even in the darkness of that day, God shined the most amazing light ever, with the restoration of my children, which after seven years was an answer to prayer. God is faithful! I will always be grateful to you for those precious moments with my children the night you died. You also have given me another gift and that is seeing what this did to everyone involved, and the aftermath of it. I will always choose and value my life and will never consider suicide again. In seeing the pain, and feeling the pain, I choose this precious gift of life that God has given me and will treasure every day and every moment, from here on out. I just want you to know from the bottom of my heart, I have totally forgiven you.

To Ronnie Bruce

This book would have never happened without your editing ability. I could never thank you enough for putting hours and hours into it for me. I pray that God will triple bless you for investing so much time into his kingdom. Thank you

Acknowledgements

To both my bosses, Michael Gee and John Gee, to the memory of their father, Mickey Gee Sr., and to my coworker Theresa Downs a.k.a. Sweet-T, all from the Pants Store.

Thank you for all the years you have put up with me and my craziness, and just for giving me so much grace while walking through some of the most difficult situations in my life. I have never seen anyone, or any company, give people who are down on their luck a chance the way you two always have. Not just to me but also to others. I have seen you hire people whose application most companies would have thrown into the garbage. But not the two of you. You gave them a chance, and they have ended up being the best employees ever. You allowed me to go through all my mess without firing me, encouraging me the whole way, and always asking me, "What can we do for you?" I am so grateful to be so blessed with such a wonderful job and to work with the most amazing coworkers ever. Just so you know, you two have been amazing bosses, and I am truly blessed to work for you both at The Pants Store.... I'm just sayin'.

To David and Missy Cooper and their families:

Wow, what a journey. I just want to take a minute to thank you for being such an example to me for the last seven years. Missy you are truly the reason why this book is being written. You were the one example for me that truly demonstrated God's grace in a way that was just impeccable. Even when I was hanging out in bars in the first years of my journey, you were always there loving me the whole way through. You never judged me at all but truly loved me right where I was. You did it so well–with nothing but the love of Christ shining so clearly through you. I remember watching you throughout my first year of being at recovery to see if you were for real or not. I did not like Christian people at that point and certainly did not trust any Christians at all. But immediately, just being around you, I knew right off the bat that you were different. There was something about you that was real, and it drew me to you like a magnet. In watching you, I saw your stability in Christ, and there was such a peace that you had, always giving Christ the credit, for that peace. I knew then that I wanted whatever it was you had. I knew it was real, and it made me want to be just like you. Missy, you are the one reason that I got saved. You made it easy for me to want Jesus. I hope you truly know what a huge part you and David have had in my progress, and there are not enough words to ever thank you enough. I am honored to have been the one to introduce the two of you to each other and to see you marry. For the last two years, David, you have truly shown me that there are real Christian men that do and will put God first in a relationship, showing me it can be done and keeping God at the center, you can and will make it. I look forward to having that one day again with whoever God has picked out for me. Notice I am claiming that he has that special someone just for me, and I am holding on to that, just like you told me. I hang on to that hope, Missy, I am trusting Christ that the next time I have a wedding in your home, it will be with that special someone that can give me no less than what the two of you share, and no less than God's best. I am honored to call you both my best friends.

To Jenny Hamlett Gates and family:

I remember us talking about when we first met. We were two years old and rolling a ball across the street. I will always treasure those memories of your sister Deborah and my sister Barbara always hanging out together. And you and I always hanging out together, playing barbies and all that fun stuff. We can never forget the time I hit you in the head with my baton, and you were dizzy the rest of the day. I will never forget your sister Jane babysitting all the time, I especially remember how much she still loved me, even after I went after her with a pair of scissors. I thank all your family for having such a huge part in my growing up.

What a journey it has been, and who would have ever thought growing up that we would ever walk down the roads together that we have? You have been there for me through it all, and you have loved me through whatever craziness was going on in my life; you were always there. You have really shown me what a true childhood friend should look like, and I thank God every day he picked you to be mine. Thank you for holding my head up when there were times I simply couldn't. You truly have seen it all, watched it all, and were there to encourage me through it all. What more is there to say? We will just have to sit back and see if there is a book number II, knowing I have my best friend to hold my hand the whole way throughout every chapter, no matter what.

To Linda Brewer:

From the time we met, you and I hit it off and we instantly became best friends. You have been such a great friend to me, and you have walked through so much with me, and I thank you for that. You went through all of the partying stage with me, walked through the process of recovery with me, and then together we embarked on the task of Alabama's Circle of Friends Ministry. Now that God has opened new doors for the two of us, I cannot wait to see together what God has laid out for our future. Thanks for hanging out with me every weekend, watching movies, going out to eat, and just for being a true friend to me, Thanks for always loving me well, right where I was. I love you.

To Sue Rich:

Sweet Sue, I am honored that you have been my sponsor and still continue to be such an inspiration to me. You walked with me, supported me, and encouraged me when most people had considered me a hopeless cause. I had been in the recovery process for quite a while and had just started my third step study, which, as you know, is a yearlong process. You agreed to be my sponsor through this one, and from the beginning, you saw me as who I am today way before I ever did. Thank you for believing in me all these years. You have really stepped up to the plate and loved me well. You helped in guiding me to see that my identity was in Christ and not from all my struggles. You helped me to find my way in learning who I was in Him and who He was in me. Wow, you had your work cut out for you, girl, but you stuck in there and never gave up on me. Thank you for standing beside me the day I went to my fathers grave. It was the first time in years since his death, and it was the day of a new beginning. What a huge day for me, and to know you were a part of it made it all the more special. I love you and look forward to many more meetings with you as we continue to share life together.

Introduction

My name is Christie. By God's grace, I am a survivor of childhood abuse: emotional, physical, and sexual. I wanted to share my life story to give others hope, and to get you to see Jesus in a way that you may have never seen him.

As we go through my journey, I want to show you what a real, true, loving relationship with Christ looks like, and I have no doubt that by the time you finish reading my book, you will certainly have seen that relationship unfold for yourself. Whatever situation you find yourself in, I want to let you know neither you nor your situation is hopeless. I wanted to share my journey with you so that you can see for yourself that as long as you're still breathing, there is hope. The one thing I want you to see as you read my story is that, yes, it is my life story, but when you get to the end, it's God that I truly want you to see. In other words, see the message, not the messenger.

Throughout my story, you will see a real, live picture of God's grace and know beyond a shadow of a doubt that hope knows your name. I have truly walked through every circumstance in life that one person could ever go through. There is nothing you could be going through that I don't understand from having been there myself. I pray that when you finish reading my book, you will be full of new life and hope. I hope you will see me, and my life, as a walking example of Jesus and that you will experience him in a whole new way.

In reading my book, you will notice that it is a little different than most. First, it neither has any chapters in it nor does it mention the name of the girl's home I was in. This is because the homes are still in business today around the country. All of them are individually owned, and some of them do have good directors. So it was important to me that you know my story but not to bash the entire program. Kind of like throwing the baby out with the bathwater.

Secondly, I do not mention any names, except for those who are closest to me, and my best friends. The reason is that all of the individuals in my story are still alive, and out of respect for everyone involved, I did not want to mention anyone's name. My book is not about any program, nor is it about any of the individuals involved. And it is not about heaping guilt or shame.

Let me try to explain why I made my decision of not having chapters in my book. I wanted you to see my life as it has happened, just raw and honest; I wanted you to see Jesus uninterrupted from beginning to the end. That would be hard to do if I had to break it down into chapters, and so I didn't. I know my life is a continuous story that has had many chapters in it and continues to have different chapters, which may mean book number II in the future. But if that is the case, I don't want to write the "chapters" or anything in between it anymore. I want my life now to be a blank sheet of paper. I guess you're wondering what I mean by a blank sheet of paper. It just simply means that I don't write my own agenda or chapters for my life anymore. Sometimes we are so busy writing out our own lives by pursuing what it is we want out of life—the biggest house, the best job, the best clothes, the best car, the best mate. Or maybe your life looks like this: you're busy making to-do lists or bucket lists, you're busy trying to fix everyone else's problems, or you're busy telling everyone else how they need to live their lives. How about staying so busy because you don't want to be alone? Or maybe you stay so busy because it is you that you hate being alone with. You simply don't like being with yourself. Just take a minute to think about how busyness shows up in your life.

You see, sweet friends, I know all too well all the scenarios above, because they happened to me. *Been there, done that, got the T-shirt.* So now, I just try to let my life be a blank sheet of paper and let God write out his plan for my life. You see, it is in all that busyness when we are really missing that special life that God has planned out for us. The life he wanted us to have all along, but because we keep planning our own lives and trying to do things ourselves in life, we miss it. We miss his original plan.

> *So let me pray with you now, before we even begin the book, that God will open your heart up to whatever it is He wants to show you through reading this book.*

Father, help us all to become blank sheets of paper every day, and let the chapters of our stories be nothing short of You. Let it be Your beginning and Your end. That You, God, will do what it is You want to do in our lives so we don't miss out on the special life You have planned for us. Lord, help us to stay out of Your way so You can write Your agenda in the chapters of our lives, and let our entire life stories end with Christ being the Alpha and the Omega, the beginning and the end, with none of our own written chapters in between, only Yours. Make our lives all about You, God, and show us how to join You in doing life with you. Amen.

I hope after you read my book that it will encourage you to reach for those goals, dreams and to live the life that God already had planned out just for you. Always remember that you will get out of this life what you are willing to put into it. Things did not just happen for me; I had to keep working, pursuing, and pushing, with one slammed door after another, one life disaster after another. I had a choice: I could either let this world and my past whip me and then lie down and quit, or choose to live life and believe all of God's promises in the word are true. So I kept pursuing and pushing, trusting God the whole way, and then it was He who started kicking doors open, one door after another.

What I am trying to emphasize to you is this: either we believe that all of God's Word is true, or we don't believe any of it at all. We can't pick and choose what part of the Bible we want to believe in and what part we don't. It should be all or nothing. I made the choice to believe it is all true when God says in Jeremiah 29:11 (NLT), "For I know the plans I have for you,' says the Lord. 'They are plans for good and not for disaster, to give you a future and a hope." I also choose to believe Romans 8:28 (NLT): "And we know that God causes everything to work together for the good of those who love God and are called according to his purpose for them." This Scripture does not say "Some" things will work out for those that love Christ; it says "All" things will work out to the good for those that love Christ. *All things* include all our situations, all our trials, all our hardships—whatever your situation is, it will work out if you love Christ.

Sometimes we tend to make things so difficult, but it is very simple: if you're still breathing, then there is hope. Once you come to realize in your own life that God's grace is enough, then that is when you will see hope and your name will be on it.

Grasp all that God has to offer. Again, thank you for reading my book. When you are done, keep passing it on, and love others well by showing them Jesus.

—Christie

My Story

I am a grateful believer in Jesus Christ, and by God's grace, a survivor of childhood abuse emotional, physical and sexual. In 2005 my brokenness brought me to my knees, but it was God's grace, His forgiveness, and His unconditional love that brought me to the realization that He is enough.

My dad was from Italy and was stationed in Germany, and this was where he met my mom. They married and moved to the States to live the American dream. Unfortunately, it ended when my parents got divorced when I was two. My father owned a nightclub, and his lifestyle consisted of bars, gambling and women. When my dad took my mom out of her stability in Germany, she too, was introduced to this same lifestyle.

My sister is three years older than I am, and had to step up to a parent role at a very young age. My dad was never a steady part of our lives, which left my mom having to work all the time to support my sister and me, which left us staying a lot with family members and friends. I learned to live with abandonment issues and feelings of insecurity at a very early age. There were some members of my father's family and his current wife at the time that had made such a big difference between my sister and me, and I never really understood why. I always believed it was because I was such a bad child, always in trouble, and never making good grades. But my sister, on the other hand, was a straight-A student, a great dancer, and an overachiever in school. We were totally opposites.

When I was eight, we moved from our family home to an apartment across town. It was shortly after we moved that the sexual abuse first took place, and it would continue over the course of the next few years.

It first started with a man who was a total stranger. I was playing at the playground near the tennis courts at our apartment complex, and a man in a white pickup truck pulled up. He proceeded to roll down his window and ask me if I could show him where the u-totem was, which, back in that day, was a grocery store and gas station. I did not know any better and got in the truck with him. I know, beyond a shadow of a doubt again, it was with God's grace that he did not kill me. Instead, once he was finished, he took me back to the tennis courts at our apartments and dropped me off.

The other incidents of sexual abuse that followed were at the hands of a family member who watched over my sister and I while my mom was at work, and then again by a parent of one of my girlfriends with whom I had gone to school. With the sexual abuse continuing for several years, I was at the point in my life where I was constantly in trouble, skipping school, and hanging out with the wrong crowd.

I remember one night specifically when my mom took me to the skating rink and dropped me off. When she would leave, we would have one of our friends who drove, pick us up, and we never went into the skating rink. We went riding around, drinking and listening to our loud music.

One night, when my friend Mike was bringing us back to the skating rink, we went around a curve too fast, and he lost control of the car. He was the one driving and had his arm on the arm rest of the door, and when we hit the tree, it jerked his door off and pulled him under the car, and he was killed instantly. There were three of us in the front seat: Mike, who was driving; my girlfriend, sitting in the middle; and me, sitting by the window. There were two other friends in the backseat of the car.

I just remember the car continuing to spin out of control, which seemed to take forever. When the car finally came to a stop, my girlfriend and I, by God's grace again, walked away without a scratch leaving the scene of the accident. We walked back to the skating rink and never told anyone that we had been in that car. A few days later, the police came to our house to question me about the accident because they had found my shoes and my purse in the floor board. It was then I had to tell my mother the truth, which scared her to death. She knew I was out of control and feared I would end up dead.

My mom had just become a Christian and had started attending church regularly, but at this point, I was already in a stage of full blown rebellion and was not going to stop now. I decided to run away with my boyfriend. His name was Larry. He was fifteen, and I was eleven almost twelve. We got one of our friends to drive us and drop us off in Memphis, Tennessee, at the bus station.

While we were at the bus station, we talked to some guy who told us about an abandoned building we could sleep in. Then a cop came up to us not knowing we were runaways. He thought we were there with our parents. The officer proceeded to tell us that he happened to know the guy that had approached us and that the guy had just gotten out of prison.

The officer said, "You two are awful lucky that I was here, because this guy would have raped you and then probably would have killed Larry." So, once again, we were totally saved by God's grace. Later that day, we talked to one of the guys who worked at the bus station, and I think he really liked us. We told him the truth that we had run away from home. He felt so sorry for us and took up a collection of money, which we used to stay in an old nasty motels and paying for our meals. Eventually, we met some guy and his girlfriend who were returning from their vacation and he offered for us to come and stay at his house. With an APB out on us, our luck eventually ran out.

One morning, we were sound asleep in the floor in the guy's living room, and we woke up to police officers standing over us. We were picked up and put in juvenile until our parents, along with the Jefferson County sheriff's department, came to pick us up. Shortly after getting out of juvenile, I was informed that I would be going to a Christian girls' home in the ghettos of Indianapolis, Indiana. I was told I would be there two weeks, and upon arrival, I was informed it was a year-plus program.

I was taken from the office and put into what they called the "hole," which was in the basement of a very old home. They took my clothes, put me in a corner and blocked it off with a roll away bed and filing cabinets. It was so cramped I did not have room to straighten out my legs. I stayed in the hole for the next four months, which included my thirteenth birthday.

During the day, I was either in the corner or scrubbing the floor with a toothbrush and at night slept on a hard, cold cement floor with nothing but a sheet. I would lie there and watch the rats run behind the washer and dryer, and see other girls tied down to rollaway beds screaming, while others were put in closets for weeks at a time. When the girls were put into the broom closet, there were so many of them that they would have to figure out how they would position themselves so they would all fit. They even had to use the bathroom in there. I just remember feeling scared to death. There were bars on all the windows, and at night, the staff slept in front of the doors on rollaway beds.

After being there a few years, I had earned outside privileges, which was going out to the shed and separating things that came in from goodwill. My friend Mindy was helping me sort through bags that had been donated to our girls' home by a lady's family that had passed away. Mindy and I were talking, and she proceeded to tell me that she could not stand being locked up anymore and informed me that she had taken all the medicine she had found in one of the bags. I went running in, screaming for help, and the counselors came and got Mindy. I remember watching them walk her up and down the hall, making her drink salt water, and sticking her head in and out of a tub of cold water. They waited so long to call for medical help that she died right in front of me, at my feet.

Neither my father nor anyone in his family ever called me, sent me a letter, or had any contact with me the whole time I was locked up at the girls' home. It was as if when I got sent away, I did not matter to any of them anymore. I guess it was "out of sight, out of mind." It was such a feeling of abandonment and one of the loneliest feelings I had ever felt in my life, just to think I lived all those years with feelings of such inadequacy and just not being lovable. What is a child to think when her own father doesn't love her?

In the back of my book you will find the voices of the survivors that were in the girls home which will give you a better idea what it was like in there. I wanted to let some of the people with whom I had reconnected have a voice. I had made a promise that if I ever wrote a book, their voices would be heard. I found a forum online several years back and found a lot of the people who were there at this particular center at the same time that I was. They had posted about their experiences there also. I did not edit anything, except remove their last names, the name of the program, the names of the directors, and the staff members' names, if they were mentioned.

I want to say thank you to each survivor for telling your story and for sharing with me your most intimate details. What I want to say to all of you is, don't ever give up. Don't let this experience keep defining you. Just remember, hope does know your name.

Now getting back to my story. After Mindy's death, I just did what I could do to be a perfect child so I could get out. Finally, right before my sixteenth birthday, I did. Shortly after I left, the directors of the girls' home were arrested and charged with child abuse. But with getting out, I was also bringing back a lot of hurt, anger and resentment towards everyone for me being locked up for so long. I felt I had lost my whole childhood. It was forever gone, and I knew I would never get it back.

After coming home, I enrolled in a Christian school, and that is where I met my first boyfriend. He was my high school sweetheart. Over the course of time, we had become sexually active, and I ended up getting pregnant. My life at home with my mom was very rocky due to me having so much hate in my heart towards her. My pregnancy caused pure panic and days of not knowing what to do, and I knew it was not going to be acceptable to anyone in his family or mine. We talked about me having an abortion because we were so young and scared to death. Eventually that is what I did.

I was faced with even more issues, and at eighteen I ended up leaving home and moved in with my boyfriend's family. When I moved in with them, they had warned us both that if they caught us slipping into each other's rooms for any reason, I would be put out. Of course we did not listen and were slipping into each other's room quite often. At eighteen years old, I found myself getting pregnant again. This time, we decided to get married and have the baby. And on May 19, 1983, my son was born.

With me being at such a young age and never having counseling for my past, the guilt and the resentment toward my husband about the abortion was unbelievable. Keep in mind I was not emotionally equipped to handle all the issues in our marriage plus having a young child. So what I would do was withdraw from the relationship rather than work through the hard stuff, because the hard stuff hurt too much. In my mind and in my world, anyone that ever loved me left, and I just assumed that one day my husband would too. But now, I wanted to be the one doing the rejecting, not the one being rejected. So I left my marriage and filed for divorce shortly after my son turned a year old.

I was still partying like a rock star at this point and going to bars. By the time son was four I met my second husband. Shortly after we met, we dated for a little over a year and then got married; I got pregnant and had a beautiful baby girl, and she too, was born on May 19, 1990, on my son's birthday. Let me just tell you, my son was not happy having to share a birthday cake with my daughter every year. But I was happier at this point in my life than I had ever been.

My fathers side of the family always questioned if my father was my real father or not, which left me feeling as if that was why I was always treated so differently. My dad had been in a motorcycle accident and was paralyzed from the neck down. He was now with his fourth wife. She had filed for divorce, and he called me and asked me if I would help in taking care of him. Reluctantly and very resentfully, I was thinking, how could you ask me to do this? And where were you all my life when I needed you? But because in my heart I still wanted to be daddy's little girl, I did.

We ended up moving him in with us, and he became my life for many, many, years. He continued in his dysfunctional lifestyle, even in a wheelchair. I wore myself out trying to take care of him and was willing to do whatever I had to do to gain his approval and acceptance. He, in return, expected me to do things that a daughter should never have to do, once again using me and emotionally abusing me.

For years I had lifted 195 pounds of dead weight. I was never trained to properly lift him, and I was required to have two major surgeries. There were many times, if he had an accident in the middle of the night, I would have to get up and clean him up, shower him, and then put him back to bed, all while caring for two small children and a husband. My son, who shared the downstairs with my dad, was getting old enough that my dad's lifestyle was taking a toll on him, and again, on me.

A male nurse that my dad had hired, was making some gestures to my son that was making my son extremely uncomfortable. Not only that, the women my father had coming over were going half-dressed or not dressed at all in front of my son to get to the bathroom. My son was also subjected to my father and his women friends' smoking pot. Several times, when my dad was not home, my son would go jump on his bed, turn the TV on, and a pornography tape would come on. With this going on all the time, it was really taking a toll on my family, and after a long discussion with my husband, I had to accept the fact that this arrangement with my dad was not going to work. It was then I knew I had to make a decision to continue either chasing a dead dream of my daddy loving me or choosing my husband and protecting my children whom I loved more than anything.

My husband and I decided that we would move and let my dad keep our house, since it had been made handicap accessible. Even now, I did not want to hurt my father, so I came up with a story. Keep in mind I was not a Christian at this point. I told my dad that my husband's job as a nuclear pharmacist had transferred to Tennessee, when in actuality, we had just moved across town. My dad had his nurse to take care of him during the day, and we had a young couple who rented the upstairs of our home taking care of him in the evening.

A few weeks later, I received a phone call that forever changed my life. The nurse told me that when he came in that morning, he had found my dad dead. I immediately went to the house, thinking by the time I got there the ambulance was going to be there and everything was going to be okay. But it wasn't. My dad was still lying in his water bed, warm, just as if he was sleeping, and I was in total shock.

Once the investigation started, my mom and I went and talked to the DA who was working on my father's case. He begin to tell us that due to my dad's condition of being a paraplegic, neither his organs nor his blood worked or flowed like ours did, and this was making it hard to get solid evidence. Even trying to pin point a time of death was impossible because of him being in a water bed and it keeping his body temperature warm.

The DA told us that they would have to make the autopsy report as inconclusive, although all the signs of his autopsy pointed to suffocation. That is what they believed happened to him, that he was smothered with a pillow. When they scraped my dad's face to see if there were fibers from the pillow, they could get nothing because someone had shaved his face after he died.

Later into the investigation, we found out that he had gone to the casino while we were gone over the weekend and had won and paid taxes on a large sum of money. Also the casino had security video being taped, which showed the nurse stealing money from my father while he was actually sitting at the poker table, and no one ever saw him doing it, other than us who viewed the security tape. It was ironic that we were left with the fact of believing that the love of his life, gambling, was probably what ended up taking his life. I guess we will never know all the truth of what happened that day or how he died or from whose hand he died. None of the money was ever found or recovered. Unfortunately, my father was never one to tell me that he loved me, so now, all I could do is wonder if I ever mattered to him or not. This was the first time in all those years that I had ever left him. The guilt of lying to him about where we were moving weighed heavily on my mind. Now he was dead. It was just too much to bear, and I felt totally responsible for his death.

In all the years of caring for him and going through his death, it had taken a toll on me and on my marriage. The more my dad would not love me, the more I craved it, and in return, I would suck the life out of my husband. I was always expecting him to fill those needs in my life that were never met from having a stable father. I had very unrealistic expectations of him and everyone around me, including living the life that I never had growing up and living it out through my daughter.

Although I had an amazing husband at the time, let me try to give you a better understanding of why I did what I did. I had never had an example of what real love truly looked like, so therefore, how would I know? In my mind, screwed up as it was, I still had this huge void in my life, and I was so starving for love. I did not see or realize the real love that was being played out by example right in front of me by my husband. I had pictured real love like the storybook *Cinderella*. You know, where I was the princess and my Prince Charming came riding in on a white horse and we had the little white picket fence and then rode off into the sunset and lived happily ever after. This is what most little girls are taught early on, so that was just the way I thought it should be, just like it is in the storybooks.

Well, I was living in real life, and it wasn't like a storybook, so I thought I was missing something. I would watch romance movies on Lifetime or Hallmark or read one of Danielle Steel's romance books—come on, ladies, you know what I am talking about. I would want that kind of storybook relationship with my husband. The reality is, that is found only in the movies, and I know that now. By this time it had gotten to the point that I did not want to love anyone anymore because it hurt too much.

The reality of my dad's death started sinking in, and that reality hit me like a ton of bricks. Now I was never going to have that father-daughter relationship that I so longed for. That was forever gone, and the irony was, not only did I feel that he had robbed me of my childhood but now that he had also ruined my life as an adult.

In the midst of all this insanity, I had been reacquainted with an ex-boyfriend after he had heard about my father's death. I ended up having an affair with him, and shortly after burying my father, I left my husband and walked out on our marriage and divorced after sixteen years of marriage.

If you will bare with me for just a paragraph, there is something I need to say to my daughter's father: Jack, I hope you realize that you are a huge part of the reason why I am writing this book. I just wanted to take a minute and dedicate a paragraph to you to thank you for all the years of the true, unconditional love that you gave me, and to thank you in advance for forgiving me, for never seeing it. Thank you for being such an example of character to me. Thank you for showing me how to be kind to others, respect others, give to others, and just overall how to be a person of truth and integrity, which you exampled greatly in our family. Thank you for tolerating all my craziness throughout the years, and I truly apologize for hurting you to the point I did. But, you know, if all of this had not happened just the way it did, I would not be the person I am today. I am just truly sorry it came at such a high, painful hurt to you, but now I can truly see how God has used this hurt for His good. You did not deserve what I did to you or our family. I thank God because of his grace, I don't have to live with guilt and shame anymore. Because Jesus did what He did for me that day on the cross, I don't have to carry the guilt and shame of my past.

Okay, thank you for bearing with me for a minute. With that being said, let's move on to the rest of my journey. The affair was short-lived,, and I continued in this cycle of insanity, and trust me, my picker was broken; I would choose to date very dysfunctional men—the bad boys, if you will. If you were to put fifty men in a room and one of them was bad, that's the one I would choose every single time. It was a cycle of love addiction and insanity (doing the same thing over and over again, expecting a different result). I just could not stop the cycle, nor could I fill the void that I had felt for so long, and the more toxic the relationship, the more I played in to it. But in my world, it seemed *something was better than nothing*.

On the Christmas of 2005, I did not get to see my children. My lifestyle had pushed everyone I ever loved or cared about away. With no one being there to love, it actually felt like a sense of being safe. No one was around to hurt me, and I started learning how to grow numb to pain. My daughter was fifteen and had gone to live with her father, and my son was living out on his own. My communication with the both of them at this point was completely shut down. They were angry with me for leaving my marriage and tearing our family apart and because of the craziness I put them both through afterward.

At that point I was starting to hit rock bottom. I was sick and tired of being sick and tired. It was New Year's Eve in 2005 when I thought I just could not take this life as it was anymore. I could not live with the guilt and shame of leaving my father, his death, leaving my marriage and not having any relationship with my family or with my children. It was at this point I started to contemplate suicide. I would sit and think for weeks about how I could wreck my car so it would look like an accident so my children could get my life insurance. I considered the kind of pills that I could take that I knew would be enough to kill me.

Sitting in the bathroom floor in a fetal position, once again I experienced God's grace: an ex-boyfriend, whom I had not spoken to in months, called to wish me a happy new year and realized there was something wrong in my voice. He actually was the one who called to get me some help. I really thank him for helping me through one of the worst times in my life, and I will be forever grateful. You never know why God puts some of the people in our lives that he does, but he knows why, and that is all that matters.

It was this same ex-boyfriend who set up a meeting with an associate pastor for me at one of our local churches here in Birmingham. When I went in to talk to the pastor, I remember just like it was yesterday telling him that I did not have the will or the want to live this thing called life anymore. I was so tired of just barely getting through life and struggling the whole way. Everything that ever mattered to me was gone: my children, my family and my friends.

I looked at the pastor and said, "Why would I want to live?"

I will never forget his answer:

> *Christie, as long as you are alive, there is hope. Girl, do you realize how much Jesus needs you here? Do you realize how much you have to offer others? It would be a shame to rob others of what God has in store for them through you. He will be using you as His tool to share Him, just wait and see.*

He continued to tell me,

"You are so unique and have something so different about yourself that I have not seen in too many people that I have met with before."

I looked at the pastor with mascara running down my face and said, "Why? Why does He love me? Why would He use me?

Don't you hear what I am telling you, all that I have done?"

He looked at me with a tear in his eye now, and said the following:

> *Christie, do you realize what He did for you so you don't have to feel guilty anymore for what you have done? Christie, look at me. Do you realize had you been the only woman here on this earth, He would have gone through everything He did and gone through all the pain He did, just for you? He would have taken that beating, He would have hung on that cross, and He would have taken those nails that were driven through His hands and feet—spat on, mocked and laughed at—if you were the only one left in this world. If it was only you standing there watching it, He would have said, "Christie, I love you so much. This is why I am suffering now so you don't have to anymore for your past. This, Christie, I am doing and going through all this just for you."*

He continued to say,

> *With that in mind, can't you start to understand that you don't have to feel guilty anymore? You don't have to feel shame anymore. He felt all that for you that day. Would you want Him to think He did that for nothing that His suffering meant nothing to you?*
> *Then you have to believe me when I tell you this: just because people are Christians does not mean there are no consequences for their actions, because*

there are. It is not going to be easy. Just remember, your children may not be speaking to you now and may never in this life, but either you believe God's Word, or you don't. His Word promises us that He will restore what you have lost seven times over; he will restore everything back to you and then some. It is doable, not easy, but if you just give Him a chance, you will see.

The pastor proceeded to tell me that if I would give God and myself a chance, then they would give me a chance by helping me to start my healing process. He told me that the church would pay for me to go to a counseling center for a year, which I did. God's grace, absolutely, and finally, I started to receive extensive counseling every week for a solid year.

After my year there was up, my counselor referred me to a local recovery program to continue my recovery process. She said it was a Christian twelve-step program for anyone with any kind of hurts, habits and hang-ups. I thought it was just a place for drug addicts or alcoholics, and I have never had a drug or alcohol problem. She assured me it was not like that at all, and we kind of laughed, wondering how I missed not having those issues of drugs and alcohol, but I never did. I don't know the answer to that question other than because of God's grace. Also with the fact that I was around the bar lifestyle my whole life, with my dad owning a bar and after all the things I saw there. I guess I never wanted to end up like that.

My first thought when my counselor and I continued to talk about it was *Oh God, not another Christian program.* I had hated God all my adult life. I never went to church, and to be really honest, I wanted nothing to do with such a cruel God. Remember, it was all these so-called Christians and Christian programs that had done some of the cruelest things I had ever seen in my life, and it had left me with a much distorted view of God. But even with that, my counselor convinced me to give it a try.

I remember the first time I walked in those doors. I needed either one good reason to live or one good reason to die. I went into share group and started listening to others sharing so openly and honestly. I saw they had struggles just like mine, some more and some less, but nevertheless there was pain, and that is the one thing that we all had in common. I remember feeling at that moment as if I was in that Christmas show "Rudolph", and I had finally found my island of misfit toys. I got saved at the recovery program and a year later got into leadership.

It was when I truly started to surrender my life and live for God, a few years into my recovery process, that Satan started to attack me the most. The recovery program that I was attending was having some problems within its leadership, and keep in mind I was not going to any church at this point; I was only attending this recovery program. So when the leadership started falling apart and I lost the sponsor that I had there, I chose not to go back to recovery.

So now I was not in recovery anymore, nor was I in church anywhere. So when all this was unfolding, my first thought was, *yep, they are just like all the other Christians I had known in my past.* And with that, I convinced myself that all this Christian stuff was not real, like I had thought it was. The bad part of my thinking here was I was looking at people instead of at God; I had put so much of myself into recovery and the people serving there and not enough in getting to know God. So now I felt people had failed me once again. I withdrew from everything and everybody and that is when I fell apart all over again.

I never went back because I did not want to get hurt anymore. I was a pro at isolating myself if someone hurt me, not dealing with it in a healthy way but shutting them out of my life altogether and never speaking to them again. Just remember, that was my pattern. Being alone was safer than taking a chance of being hurt, not realizing that people are human and are going to make mistakes, just as it happened there. But I bailed out instead of walking through it.

You know, Satan knows where we are seamed, and he will do whatever it takes to rip that seam open. You can rest assured that wherever your weakness is, that is usually where he is going to try and rip you open the worst. I was getting so bad again and depressed to the point it was like a tape was playing over and over in my head, then rewound and played again. This is what it was playing: "Come on, Christie, you're never going to change. You are who you are. You're stuck, and you're hopeless. If you change any of this about yourself, who will you be?"

Being a new Christian, I was just not strong enough at this point to know how to deal with it, and in the midst of it all, I started to question myself: what was the point of all of this? My hurts and my habits had taken years to develop, and they had really started at my childhood. So even though they were painful and self-defeating, I held on to them because they were so familiar. Kind of like an old, comfortable pair of shoes: they may have big holes in the soles, allowing our feet to get wet, but we hang on to them because we are used to them and they are comfortable.

My character defects were like my old shoes; they were comfortable. Because I had them for so long, I had a hard time letting them go. All I ever wanted was unconditional love, for someone to love me just for me, and for who I was as a person on the inside. I always said that I wanted to marry someone that was blind, because they would never know what I looked like on the outside. I knew that in all my relationships in my past, that is what they were all based on—what was on the outside. Not that I am all that and a bag of chips, but you get the picture.

My whole life and in all my relationships, that is all I ever felt I was to anyone, with the exception of my daughter's father. Let me explain: when I was with him, my drug of choice for numbing my pain from all the hurt was food. When we met, I had always been so little, around 140 pounds, and I am 5'7". That was not the case with him throughout the majority of our marriage, yes, I was extremely overweight which began a few years after we married to the tune of, let's just say, well, over 200-plus pounds (you know I can't tell the whole weight. Girls don't tell their weight). Just sayin'.

The only reason I am sharing this is to encourage others who feel hopeless about never losing weight. You have to have the want to and start making a choice to live a whole new lifestyle, with healthy food choices and some exercise. When that cake comes around the table, you have to make a choice—yes or no. It is all about the choices we make, because it is by the choices that we are making our life what it is. When I was being tempted by good, fattening food, I would just say "No, thank you" and would make the choice to keep my eye on the goal, not on the moment.

Now there are all kinds of healthy choices out there in order to eat healthy. I did start walking around the block, but I was not working out in the gym; nothing like that. So if I can do it, you can too. I now weigh 140 pounds—yep, by God's grace and Him giving me the discipline to do it. So yes, I conquered that too, and with that, I want to encourage all my readers who are uncomfortable with your weight: you *can* do it!

Okay, let me get back on track and back to the story. I did not mean to get off on weight loss, but I guess God knew, while I was writing, someone needed that encouragement.

I had already made a mess out of my life, and the damage had already been done. I started thinking this way and believing it and then just resorted to the fact

I was who I was, and that would never change, and neither would my past. And with that, I just gave up.

I went back to what was familiar to me, which was the bar scene. At least in that environment I felt a sense of belonging and at least felt like I was somebody.

At this point, it had been ten years since I had left my marriage. I had gotten into a very deep depression. Once again, I found myself in a very bad place in my life and met someone in a bar. I figured a man in this environment, and that type of lifestyle was all I ever deserved and it was all I would ever have, because what decent man would have anything to do with me because of my past? I wanted so bad just to be loved.

Although I knew it was wrong from the very beginning, by that I mean there were signs before we married I should have taken heed to but I didn't, and I settled, and we got married. I knew it was the same thing in this relationship as it had been about in all my previous relationships, which was all about sex. But in my mind, and in what I believed once again, something was better than nothing. All I ever wanted was for him to love me, but I knew from the beginning that he didn't, he didn't know how. After a month of us being married, I found myself begging him just to call me, or to spend time with me. He was always in front of the TV, and I was always alone in the bedroom. I was constantly trying to show him how to live the right way, do the right thing, treat people the right way, respect other people, handle his finances, pay his bills on time. I was always worried if he was lying to me again or not. I was trying to encourage him to go to church, and very quickly, it was wearing me out.

Financially, he had not been honest with me. Right after we married, I started to uncover that he was on the verge of losing everything, which he eventually did. The mortgage was behind three months, and they foreclosed on our home. The car that he had given me to drive when we married had to be returned to the dealership, which I had to do. I had to handle all of this for him, and it was just too overwhelming.

I have had to be the strong one all my life, and now, I wanted to be with someone who was strong, someone that I could lean on, and that just was not happening. I sure did not have the energy now to try and change someone else into the kind of person I thought they should be. I was trying to make him into the man I wanted him to be, and he was just not interested, and it was making us both miserable.

I finally just gave up. Six months later, I found myself signing divorce papers once again. But even with him, I learned things God wanted me to learn, and I do believe that God put him in my life for a reason. He did have two of the sweetest children, and I loved them to death, and still do to this day.

Don't get me wrong here. I don't want you to think he was a bad person, because he wasn't. There was a lot of good in him too; he just had a lot of his own dysfunction from his past to deal with. I really do think he wanted to love me but just did not know how, and that is what I needed the most. I have to say, though, he did raise his two children and did a wonderful job at that. They were so respectful and so loving to me, and accepted me right off the bat.

He did really well with them. His precious daughter went on to nursing school, and his son started college also, and they are both doing well. The both of them have such a story to tell from their childhood, and I am still amazed at how grounded they are with everything they have had to go through. I admired the fact that he stepped up to the plate for them when they were just a few years old and continued to do so until they were grown, and doing it all on his own after their mother left them.

Let me just say this: I did not regret marrying him because when I left him it was this situation that God used to bring me back to my knees, and once again, back to Him, right where I needed to be. This marriage was one incident where I decided to follow my own plan and not wait on his plan, and afterward, there were consequences of a bad choice. My prayer is that in the short time we were together that he saw a little bit of Jesus, and I hope that the seed that was planted will grow, where they, too, will know God in a mighty way.

Once again, I was all alone and back on my own. But oddly, it was in these alone times when I realized it became less of me and more of God. I know all singles can relate exactly to what I am talking about. When there is no one else when you get home, no one to sit down and have dinner with, no one there to hold you at night and tell you it will be okay, it is in those times when we start to seek Him the most. But with nothing but time on my hands, I had plenty of time to think, and all the things I had previously learned at recovery just kept playing in my mind, and I just couldn't forget about it. So I thought, *what the heck, I would give it another try.*

I started attending the same recovery program again and worked my restoration period back into leadership. I started another step study, which is a year long process, and this was my third. I know it takes some of us longer to get it than others, but I truly believed this time that I had to get to the root of my problems. I had to learn not to just see the dysfunction that I was living in, but also to start gaining an understanding of what was causing it. It wasn't my behavior up until today that was the problem. It was the root of the problem which had started way back.

In that same year, I decided to fast from TV and secular radio for a year. I only wanted good in, good out. In other words, in the car, I listened to worship music. At home, I would get ready in the morning with worship music. Other times I would read, study God's Word, or just whatever. But for a solid year, that was what I did, and trust me, when I was putting nothing but good in, good was what started coming out. I finally started to recognize that I was not worthy, but God has made me worthy.

Now I was starting to realize that the emotional script God originally had given me had been extremely tainted by my life experiences and the circumstances that had happened to me throughout my life. But now I can say that by God's grace, these scripts are no longer what I live by, nor do those tainted emotions identify who I am anymore. They do not hold captive my responses or my reactions anymore. And yes, some of those messages were true, and some were false. But the problem was, being so young then, I didn't have the ability or what it took to edit those messages, so I went through life believing them all to be true.

With this realization, for the first time in my life, I started being honest with others and myself. I began to open up, and I was fortunate enough to have a sponsor by my side who prayed with me, loved me and accepted me for who I was, right where I was. She listened to me, encouraged me, and more than anything never judged me. She extended so much of God's grace to me and gave me hope that I did not have to live in insanity anymore. Never living a healthy lifestyle or knowing what that even looked like, it was all new to me, but I was willing to learn.

My best friend, Missy, whom I met at recovery, was a huge influence in my process. When I first met her, she had such a sweet presence about her, one of those people you just love being around. I will always remember, no matter how much I was going through, she always loved me right through it all. Even when I was going back to the bars the first time I left recovery, she would say to me,

> *Christie, if you drink too much, please call me to come and get you. I don't care what time it is. I love you and do not want you to get hurt. God loves you, Christie, and he has big plans for you, and it is not in this bar lifestyle.*

She was always so kind, never harsh or judging, but so loving and so giving of herself, just a living, walking example of God's grace to me. Missy was showing me through what she was doing with me, how to love others well.

As Missy continued to extend grace to me so many times, I started seeing what she had was so real. She truly walked out Jesus to me. When she would talk to me about how much Jesus loved me, I would see the peace and presence she had about her. I truly started wanting whatever it was that she had. I never saw her waver at all. Even when she was walking through a divorce, she still hung on to Jesus and trusted him the whole way through. She never thought of herself but always about others and how they were doing. Her stability in her walk with the Lord was incredible and very contagious. Her stability and consistency in my life was huge for me because that was the first time I had stability in someone. It was like a breath of fresh air for me. Finally, after all these years, I felt now that I had Missy, which was that one person in my life I could open my heart to and learn how to trust again.

I made a promise to God that if ever He would give me the contentment and peace that Missy had, I would do anything and everything I could to help others find it also. I promised Him that I would be a tool that He could use and would try my best to be a living example for Christ, extending grace to others just as Missy had done for me.

The Bible speaks of it as an action and attitude, not just an emotion. Love is a by-product of our new life in Christ. Please see Romans 5:5 and 1 Corinthians 13. Christians have no excuse for not loving, because Christian love is a decision to act in the best interest of others.

But the Holy Spirit produces this kind of fruit in our lives: love, joy, peace, patience, kindness, goodness, faithfulness…" (Galations 5:22, NLT)

I just love the part of the Scripture that love is a decision to act in the best interest of others, which is exactly what Missy did in my life. This is just to give you an example of how God works in different situations, and also to push you a little more to think about some of your own situations that you may face on a daily basis. When you see people out in public that may be different, ask yourself, *Do I love them well?* You know, those individuals with tattoos and piercings all over their bodies, or maybe someone with that purple hair sticking up like a cockatoo, or someone all dressed in black, or someone with a nose ring—or just however they may be different or, what we assume is different. I am sure they look at us like we are different. What if they are normal and we are the ones who are different? Ever thought about that? We, as Christians, should be different, and this is why. This will give you something to think about, so the next time you see someone *different* and before you are so quick to judge them, ask yourself, "Am I loving others well?"

This was one of those "aha" moments for me. My daughter Katie has tattoos and piercings also, and yes, everywhere she goes—let's just say, for simplicity sake, to Wal-Mart after church, it is mainly those dressed in their Sunday best that you know just came from church who give her that snarled look the most. I should know. I have stepped back and watched it firsthand.

One day, Katie and I were sitting at home in our rocking chairs on the front porch, and I asked her, "Katie, why all the tattoos? Why all the piercings?"

She said to me, "Mom, while you wore all your pain on the inside, I wear my pain on the outside."

I have never forgotten that to this day. That was such a profound moment for me. That totally changed my outlook on others who chose to be different, and now I love them well, right where they are. Besides, is that not what Christ would do?

I remember the first time I took Katie with me to a recovery meeting. When it was over and we went to the car, she said, "Wow, this is the first place I have been as far as 'church' stuff is involved, where people don't judge you or look at you like you're a loser."

I thought that was the saddest thing I had ever heard. If Katie thinks that way, I am assuming a lot of other people feel that way too. If that is the case, we really need to start looking at our churches. Remember, each one of us, we are the church, so we really need to start looking within ourselves. We need to look at our actions toward others and how our attitudes are to each other and ask ourselves the question "Do we love others well?" If not, we need to change it quickly.

Listen really close to what Katie said here. She did not say that was the first *bar* she had walked in where people treated her differently. She said that was the first *church* she had walked in, and to think she is referring to Christians in the church. That was really sad. It was really cool, though, to see God working through this. After a few times of Katie watching how she was being treated at recovery and seemingly being amazed that people accepted her for who she was as a person and didn't judge her for her tattoos and piercings, her eyes were fully opened. Trust me, she was watching, just as I did in my early walk with the Lord. She was watching not only those at recovery but also my best friend, Missy, who exampled Christ as well for Katie as she had for me.

Then the last time before Katie moved to Huntsville, she came to another recovery meeting with me. After a large group, I started off to our gender-specific share group and noticed neither Katie nor Missy came in behind me. Because I was leading that share group that night, I could not get up and go look for them.

After share group was over, I went to look for Katie and Missy. Missy stopped me in the hall to tell me that when Katie was coming out of large group and saw Missy at the door, Katie grabbed her and Art—who was the ministry leader there at the time—and asked them to pray with her to accept Jesus in her heart. So they took Katie somewhere else to meet with her and led her to the Lord.

I was beyond thrilled and just thought, *Wow, how cool God is, and wow at how he works.* I was just in awe of God at that moment, and there was nothing I could say other than "Thank you, Jesus, thank you."

As Christians, it seems people do tend to watch us more. Even though we are Christians, Christ never said we would never walk through tough situations or circumstances sometimes. He just said He would be there to get us through them. But sometimes as we are going through these tough times, we let our circumstance or situation turn our hearts hard, being angry at God, harboring bitterness and resentment. The truth is that sometimes we have to walk through situations and circumstances that are not too comfortable, realizing that serving Christ is not always comfortable. But let me say this: I am sure when He hung on that cross, it was not too comfortable for Him either. So if He can go through what He did for us, we can take some suffering here on this earth and go through whatever it is we are going through, trusting Him that He will bring us through it.

I started remembering what that pastor had said to me early on, about what I would be doing for other people. He was right. Because now, it is important to me to help others see that their identity is not in their past or in what they have done but in Christ, in His grace and His hope.

You see, sometimes I am still faced with some of the same problems and some of the same struggles. I realize that just because I am a Christian now, it does not fix everything, nor does it make my life all okay. I still have to live with the consequences of my actions and the poor choices that I had made. The big difference now is my identity is in God, not in my past. I no longer have unrealistic expectations of myself or of others, nor do I carry guilt and shame anymore. This time, I finally believe that Jesus has forgiven me, which was huge for me. In return, I have learned how to start forgiving myself and others who have hurt me, and that was how my healing process truly began. I have always heard that unforgiveness is like you drinking poison and expecting the other person to die.

Colossians 1:22-23 (NLT) says the following:
22 Yet now he has reconciled you to himself through the death of Christ in his physical body. As a result, he has brought you into his own presence, and you are holy and blameless as you stand before him without a single fault.
23 But you must continue to believe this truth and stand firmly in it. Don't drift away from the assurance you received when you heard the Good News. The Good News has been preached all over the world, and I, Paul, have been appointed as God's servant to proclaim it.

> *The way to be free from sin is to trust Jesus Christ to take it away. We must stand firmly in the truth of the good news, putting our confidence in Jesus alone to forgive our sins, to make us right with God, to empower us to live the way he desires. When a judge in a court of law declares the defendant not guilty, the person is acquitted of all the accusations or charges. Legally, it is as if he or she had never been accused. When God forgives our sins; our record is wiped clean. From his perspective, it*

is as though we had never sinned. God's solution is available to you. No matter what you have done or what you have been like. God's forgiveness is for you.

I would like to encourage you to look up the bible verse Colossians 1:22-23. Then list those things you are still beating your self up over and that you feel are why you don't deserve God's mercy. It really helps to get it out of your head and on paper.

Have you come to terms with the fact of God's forgiveness?

Are you still beating yourself up over your past sins and thinking you are undeserving of God's mercy?

A few years ago, in going through my recovery process, I went with my sponsor, Sue, and three of my best friends—Missy, her now-husband, David, and

Linda. They went with me to my father's grave. I had not been there since he died in 1998. I read him a six-page letter of everything that I felt he had done to me that had hurt me my whole life. Every person that was there with me was crying as I finished reading the letter. Each one of them took a turn to pray.

After they all finished praying, I looked up, and it was right at sunset. The sun was going down, tears were streaming down all of our faces, and there was the most beautiful ray of light in the back of that sunset. It was at that moment, on that day, that I knew that I had truly forgiven my father. I buried the letter at his grave, and that was when my true healing began. Something in me changed that day.

As for my mother, I love her now more than ever. She is my best friend. She has been able to share with me what all she had to walk through, even living through the war. It ranged from their home being bombed, to her surviving starvation, to the point she had a hole in her lung. She is the seventh of eight children, and her father was a dentist in the village where they lived in Sterbfritz, which is near Frankfurt, Germany.

Growing up, my mother was never allowed to show any kind of emotion. She doesn't remember her father ever telling her he loved her. So because of her lack of feeling loved and never seeing an example herself within her family, it was hard for her to know anything different than what she was taught. Unless you are taught any different—or go through a lot of hard work by choice, like what I did—then unfortunately you grow up as a product of your environment.

My grandfather was by no means a bad man, just a very strict one. Because of her father's firm hand, my mother learned how to be emotionless and just tried her best to always be a good girl. She had to act and wear that mask as if everything was okay; she was not even allowed to cry because her father would tell her that showed weakness. On the other hand, he had a very kind side to him, too, as you will see.

She is also in the process of writing her own book. It will be called "Father, forgive them," and I look forward to that journey for her in the future.

Here is the introduction to her book which will show you some of her story.

My father, Zahnarzt Reinhard, was one of the unsung heroes of WWII. Please allow me to share his story with you. I hope that it will touch your heart as it has touched the hearts of others.

Though I was a child, the memories of those war torn years are indelibly imprinted in my mind. Our family lived across the street from the railroad station in our home which was also my father's office in the village of Sterbfritz, Germany. I can still remember watching my Jewish friends being loaded on the train like animals... I cannot help but remember the fear and confusion in their eyes as they departed for Dachau... However, I also remember the anger and resolve in my father's eyes.

My father and another man were the only dentists for our village and the surrounding area, and because our house was also close to a coalmine that used the forced labor of Jews, and Belgium and French prisoners, my father's services were often called upon. The soldiers would frequently bring these prisoners by truck to have their teeth pulled, specifying that no anesthetic be used (the prisoners suffered from a severe gum disease resulting from malnutrition).

Now, my father was a very tough man with a hard exterior. Furthermore he carried himself with great confidence and authority, especially in the presence of the Nazis, Hitler's Gestapo, and the SS troops (With the horrors of war all around us, this was one of the ways he used to cover for his real activities, which were helping dying Jews and war prisoners). So when the German soldiers brought the Jews into my father, he would make a big scene in their presence. What an actor he was! He would bitterly tell them that he did not want these Jews in his waiting room. Then he would command the prisoners to go downstairs into the cellar, because he would not tolerate "dirty Jews" sitting with his patients. With that, the guards would be satisfied and leave their charges to their supposed "tormentor". They would then head off to a nearby gasthaus .

Much to the prisoner's relief, once the guards were gone, they found in the dreaded cellar the comforts of food, clothing, and a genuine break from their real tormentors. At least for a few hours, they could strengthen themselves with some nourishment and tender care.

One day, during this time, a Jewish attorney came into our garden where my father grew lettuce, onions, leaks, etc. His eyes were hollow and he appeared to be starving to death. I remember that he looked at my father and said, "Dr. Reinhard, could I have just one of your leeks? I am so hungry." My father told him, "No, you cannot have just one leek, but you can fill your pockets full and put lettuce or anything else you want in your pockets." The Jews sewed secret pockets inside their coats so they could hide things from their oppressors.

Sadly, the Gestapo found out what my father was doing, and one day the SS served my father with an official Summons to appear in Dachau where he was to be executed. A patient of his, a Baroness, helped him by calling a close friend of hers who also happened to be one of Hitler's generals. She asked the general not to execute her dentist—her personal dentist—who was the only dentist who was able to help her with a gum disease from which she suffered. This fortuitous call saved his life!

Although my father faced death and suffered through tremendous persecution, he still reached out to the Jews and war prisoners by helping them escape and by secretly taking care of them. Then in 1945, the game was finally up and the SS ordered the hanging of our family! Indeed, we surely would have been hung had it not been for the fact that the Americans had pushed to within only an hour of our little village. Thankfully, in the ensuing chaos, our lives were spared!

After the war, my father continued as a dentist. He passed away in 1991 at the age of 97. His legacy of love continues on in the lives of his family members and the children of the Jews and other prisoners he selflessly helped. My father was a living testimony to the faithfulness of God's Word. He lived according to what is written in Torah where God promised Abraham:

And I will bless them that bless thee, and curse them that curse thee; and in thee shall all families of the earth be blessed.

My father believed this and so do I!

Rosemarie R. Musso

My mom has overcome so many obstacles of her own.

Coming to the States, she could not even speak English. My dad left her with two children, and she was left with no family here to support her and had to do it all on her own. She is a Holocaust survivor, and at sixty-three, she went to law school, and she is still practicing here in Birmingham to this day. She never gave up and never quit trying to better herself and to make her children's lives better.

God has totally restored our relationship better than it has ever been, and my mother is truly my inspiration and my hero. And please, when her book is released, buy it; you will not want to miss her whole story. It is truly amazing.

Now let's continue on my journey. I continued to walk through my healing process, and by choice, decided not to date for the next three years. I wanted to really work on me, and really get to know the Lord on a personal level and really take time to study and learn who I was in Him and who He was in me. For the first time in my life, I was content, and I finally liked being with me. I can honestly say that now I did not feel like I needed a man to complete me anymore. I was pouring myself into my singles ministry and had just taken a new position as the singles minister at a new church that had just started in Mountain Brook here in Birmingham.

While staying totally committed to God in the process and putting Him first in every area of my life, I met a very special man that God brought into our ministry. He started attending our singles ministry after his divorce, and we hit it off immediately. We were like two kids again, staying up all night on the phone, or he was at my house every day after he got off work. He had been coming to our ministry for a few months, and over the course of spending time with him and getting to know him, we started dating. Just within a few months, we were together all the time. I was so happy again, and it just felt so right. We knew our meeting was nothing short of being God ordained due to all the circumstances that led him to our particular ministry. I had total peace, with no question that he was the one for me.

We started talking about getting married at which time we started doing premarital counseling with our pastor. Now with me being a Christian and being in ministry, and with him being the first Christian guy I had ever dated, it was extremely important to me not to have sex with him before we were married. I did not want to repeat past behaviors, and in my past, this was the area where I always struggled. But now, I was determined to do it God's way.

We had originally planned to marry on New Year's Eve, but some of our situations were changing very quickly. My mom had to have hip replacement surgery, and this one was going to be her sixth surgery after a failed hip replacement she had several years ago. The doctors were concerned if the surgery was even going to work or not because so much of the bone in her hip had deteriorated. If the surgery didn't work, it would leave her in a wheel chair. We knew there was a possibility, depending on the outcome of the surgery, that she might have to stay with me for a while. Also within the same week of her surgery, my lease was up on my apartment. My fiancé did not want me to sign another six-month lease. Our original plan was for me to move in with my best friend, Missy, for the next four months until we got married.

My fiancé said the following:

> *Christie, there is no sense in paying to move you twice in a matter of 4 months. If we go ahead and get married now, I can help with your mom and she can stay here at the house with us after her surgery.*

We were also worried that if we had waited until New Year's Eve, my mom may have not been in any condition to do the wedding, and it was important to both my fiancé and I that she be the one to marry us. It was her marrying us that made it that much more special. Also I was determined to stay abstinent until we got married, and we did. The truth was that my fiancé had really been increasingly pressuring me to be more physically involved, and I was afraid to talk to anyone about it because I did not want anyone to think badly of him. I was so afraid that because of my past I was going to cave in at some point and mess up everything that I had been working so hard for the last seven years. In my mind, I just kept going back to what my pastor had told me about what the Bible said about this, that "it is better to marry than to fall into sexual sin."

My fiancé just kept on and on, pushing for us to go ahead and get married, and with that, I finally agreed, and we did. Both of us felt in our hearts that it was so God ordained, and on August 7, we were married. My sweet mother was able to marry us, and we were so excited, although she had to stand up with a walker and was in a lot of pain in both of her hips; and she was only a week away from her scheduled surgery. But I was thrilled beyond belief because my now-husband was the first man that I had ever dated that my mom had ever felt good about, and really felt as though God had put him in my life. I just knew God was going to honor us for honoring him in every way of our lives together. We chose, first and foremost, to honor Christ in our decision, and overall, that was what was most important to the both of us. We knew we had to do what would be most pleasing to him because ultimately, he is the only one you ever have to worry about pleasing, not other people, and I know we did that.

I was still traveling a lot and sharing my testimony. Shortly after we were married, I was asked to go to Nicaragua to speak at several churches and to do some women's conferences there, and I did. I was so happy and would share with everyone there about how God could and did restore to me everything that I had lost and then some, just like that pastor told me He would.

I was truly happier now than I had been in a long time. I had the love of my life, and he was a Christian man who truly loved the Lord, and always came across to others to be so happy.

Although I was very happy and I loved my husband so much, he, on the other hand, had some very unfortunate situations going on in his life that were affecting him in a very negative way. Let me try to explain that a little: Prior to us getting married and even after we married, some of the people that were closest to my husband were very angry at him for us getting married as quickly as we did.

I did not know until after we got married about some of the conversations that had taken place between those individuals and my husband. I had very little communication with these individuals prior to us getting married. Some of them I had not even met—not by my choice but theirs. I tried on several occasions before my husband and I got married to meet with them, but they said they were not ready to meet me. So with that being said, I did not even try anymore because I did not want anyone to feel like I was pushing myself on them. I tried to respect them right where they were with all this.

What little communication I did have with them was through a few Facebook messages. I knew by the messages I had received from them that they were angry. They expressed their anger toward me in some of their messages, that I will just say, were not very nice at all. Their messages to me completely caught me off guard; I was just simply not expecting it.

After talking with my husband about it, I tried to keep in mind what he told me, that they were just hurting because of him getting married again. I truly did not know of all the other things that were going on between my husband and all of the individuals involved at the time. My husband kept every bit of that from me before we married, and even after we married. I think he was just trying to keep from hurting me any further concerning all those situations. He would always tell me that he was afraid that I would leave him because of the drama, and because of how some of them were acting. I know he had that in his mind a lot because he would tell me that over and over again. I figured that was why he did not share a lot of what was going on with me. In my mind, I just figured it would eventually work itself out due to me being in that same situation in the past, and it always ended up working out. All I could really do at this point was to trust my husband in what he had told me, which was this:

> *Christie, I know these individuals a lot better than you do, so just trust me when I tell you it will work itself out, and just don't worry about it. He said they will all get to know you and see*

who you are and what kind of person you are, and eventually will love you to death.

But needless to say, that never happened. Now I do realize I should have paid more attention to the extent of the seriousness of each of these situations with all the individuals involved, and would have, had I known the extent of it all. I would have tried to work it out with them before we ever married, but I didn't. When no one was there to support him at our wedding, I was really surprised, up to the minute I said "I do." I kept asking him why they were not coming.

That was when he finally told me some of what had happened when he told them we were getting married. He proceeded to tell me there had been some very hurtful communication between him and all the individuals involved, and that they were not coming because we had moved our wedding up so quickly.

I remember feeling so bad for him that night because all my family, my children and my friends were there. We did have a beautiful small wedding, but it was very special, and we married at my best friend Missy's house. We honeymooned in New York for a week and were having the best time of our lives.

We went through Central Park in a horse and carriage, had pictures made on the bridge where they made the movie *You've Got Mail*. I remember him telling me standing on that bridge, "Christie, our love story is going to be a millions time better than that movie. I just know it."

I remember then riding through Central Park, and that was the first time that I had noticed that he had a bottle of medication in his pocket. I had never seen him with it before, and I asked him why he was carrying the whole bottle of medication. He said he had been on Lortab and muscle relaxants for years due to a shoulder injury from playing football. He told me he did not take more than two Lortab and two muscle relaxants a day, and so I remember asking him, "If you just take four pills a day, why do you carry the full bottle around?" That just struck me kind of odd, and then I asked him, "Does that not bother you, having that big pill bottle in your pocket?" He said no, so I believed him and his explanation and just did not mention it again.

After leaving New York and upon returning home, we started getting all my stuff moved in. He was excited about me decorating the house he had just bought. We were finally getting settled and getting the house finished and both of us were learning how to get used to each other's quirks. You know how it is when you go from being single to moving in with someone; there is just an adjustment period. We were like two school kids. I remembered calling my mother every morning on the way to work and telling her, "Did you know I have the best husband in the world?"

Just a few months after we married, these relationships with each of these individuals in my husband's life continued to not improve as fast as he thought they should. At this point, I started noticing some changes in his behavior. He would be the sweetest, kindest, most loveable man in one minute, and then, within a matter of seconds, he was someone else. He could go from type a personality to type z personality within a matter of minutes. If I made him mad about the littlest thing, he would say he was going to divorce me. He knew that I struggled with abandonment issues from my past, and that is where he would choose to hit me the worst. Trust me, it was torture for me every time he threatened to leave me, and I would feel so overwhelmed with fear.

Each week, we continued to meet for counseling with our pastor and with another professional counselor that our pastor had recommended us to see. When we would go to our appointment and I would tell them that he had threatened divorce again, they would ask my husband, "Why do you do that, knowing that is what hurts her worst? Why do you threaten to leave her every time she does the littlest things wrong?"

He would respond with the following:

> *I don't mean to. I don't want to do it. I am just so full of anger and bitterness towards all these other individuals who have hurt me. I guess all the anger from my past is spewing over on her because I have not ever dealt with it, until now.*

He would cry and apologize to me profusely until the next time. It was almost like he really could not help it, to the point it was really starting to concern me because I knew that that was not the man I married. Our pastor told me, "Christie, I do not know what else to do. I have asked him time and time again to take the divorce card off the table when you upset him, and he just will not do it."

So we continued our counseling sessions. We were in the counselor's office one day with the pastor and the counselor, and they asked my husband if he would be willing to go to a doctor of their choice just to get checked out. At this point, I had already been telling them both I felt there was a prescription-pill problem. They, too, felt something more was going on with my husband, but his response to them every time it was questioned was no.

Prior to meeting me, my husband had dealt with drug issues with another individual who was in his life, and he had dealt with it for years. That was the one reason no one would have ever believed he was doing the same thing, because of how bad he would tell us he hated anything that had to do with prescription medication, because of what he had been through. He told the counselor he would not go to their doctor but that he had a good doctor whom he had been going to for years, and he would go see him within the next week.

My husband and I discussed it in length, and he agreed that he would go to his doctor the following week, and he did. It was then, after multiple testing procedures, that he was diagnosed with having a bipolar disorder. He also had been diagnosed with clinical depression. I started to notice the depression getting worse, and in that time, he was getting up a lot during the night and getting into the medicine cabinet.

We continued meeting with our counselor and our pastor each week, just trying to walk through not only a new marriage but also with all these issues on top of it. Every week we went, I would keep saying to the counselor and to our pastor, "I think my husband is abusing prescription medication." But time and time again, he would continue to deny it, and with that, there was nothing they could do. I knew it; I just had that gut feeling you feel when you know something is not right but you just can't put your finger on it. Several times, when his behavior got so drastic, I would ask him what he had taken.

One particular incident that stood out was one Saturday morning. My son was leaving on military duty again, and we were going to the airport to see him off. My husband was freaking out about going by his office to pick something up. I said, "Can't it wait till we leave the airport?"

He said, "No, it will just take me a few minutes to run in."

So we went. We pulled up to where he worked. He put his ID key card in to get into the parking deck, and it would not work. He was acting like he was starting to panic and getting so agitated that we could not get into the building. So he called another employee that was working there that day, and he told my husband he had run up the road to get breakfast but had left the back door propped open and that my husband could get in the building that way.

The employee said, "Don't you remember? They had to shut the power off to the building today to do some type of maintenance."

My husband said, "Oh yeah, I remember now. I just completely forgot."

So we went around to the back door, which was propped open, and we were the only ones in the building. He was showing me around the courthouse and telling me what all he did there, and even took me and showed me where he worked out in the gym every morning. Then we went into his office, which was pitch black because there were no windows in there, and remember, the power was off.

It was so dark. He told me to stand outside the door and hold it open for him so he could have a little bit of light from the windows that were in the front of the courthouse so he could get what it was he needed. Then I heard him trying to open a cabinet with a key. He said he could not see the key hole and could not get it open because it was so dark. I told him I would use the light of my cell phone so he could see what he was doing, so I found something to prop the door open, and I went in there with him. He opened the cabinet, and there was a full bottle of Lortab and another bottle of muscle relaxants.

I looked at him and said, "This is what you could not wait to come and get?" I was anxious to get to the airport so I didn't miss my son leaving. I asked my husband, "Why do you have this medicine down here? If you don't have a problem with them, why are they not at home?"

I knew he had a bottle at home, besides that one at work, because I had seen it that morning in his briefcase. I remember asking him, "You work in a federal court house and they don't care if you have this medication in here? Will you not get in trouble?"

It was at this point once again I told our pastor, "I am for sure really feeling now that my husband has a prescription pill problem."

Another incident occurred when I came back from Nicaragua. One Sunday afternoon, my husband was upset with something that had gone on and had locked himself in the bedroom. He was hollering through the door, that he was fixing to take the whole bottle of pills. I was so scared, I remember beating on that bedroom door, shaking like a leaf, and telling him I was calling the police if he did not open the door. He finally opened the door and said if I ever called the police, he would lose his job. I told him, "Threatening suicide and scaring me like that was not okay. When you are threatening to kill yourself, I am not really concerned about your job."

The next day, we went to meet with our pastor and counselor. I told them what my husband did, and when they asked him why he did that, he said, "I just wanted to scare her."

By this point, he was taking five to six different medications. Once again, I had no idea he was taking all this. He was on Lortab, which was being prescribed by several different doctors; Ambien, which is for sleeping; Cymbalta, which is for depression; Methocarbamol, which is some type of muscle relaxant; and Alprazolam, which is the generic to Xanax, which slows down the movement of chemicals in the brain that may become unbalanced. This results in a reduction in nervous tension (anxiety). Alprazolam is used to treat anxiety disorders, panic disorders, and anxiety caused by depression. Plus he would throw in about seven to eight over-the-counter Benadryl every day on top of all that.

I was sitting at his desk one day at home while he was at work and had found some emails that had been exchanged between him and the individuals he was having problems with. It was after reading them I started to realize how bad this situation really was, and how it was affecting him and how bad he was truly hurting.

At this point, and knowing a little more now from reading some e-mails, I did decide—without him knowing about it—to reach out a few times to all the individuals involved. I had called them on the phone several times, reached out to them by email and Facebook messaging and in person. I contacted them to let them know how bad it was hurting my husband not having them in his life and being in a position to have to make a choice between loving me and having a relationship with them. I even asked them if there was anything I could do. I told them I could not change the past, and even though we had married sooner than they would have liked, I was willing to change our future together. I asked them to please try to understand that we truly believed we were doing it God's way and were really trying to honor God in the process of it all.

I told them I was sorry that I had any part in hurting them and really wanted my husband to have them back in his life. Therefore, what could I do to make that happen? Whether they ever accepted me or not, I shared with them how much he loved them and how much this was hurting him, but they just were not ready to move on and restore those relationships with him just yet.

In this conversation with them, they began to tell me it was not about me or our marriage that upset everyone, but the way my husband went about telling them and handling things. They told me they loved him more than anything, but it was just going to take some time for them to heal, which I totally understood. I knew it was totally okay for people to handle things differently than others, and that is why God made us all different and unique. It did not make their decision bad or wrong because they were not ready to do that as quickly as he thought they should. I knew they would eventually work it out when they felt they were ready. I just took my hands off the situation and asked God to take over and be in control of fixing all this mess, and to help me take my hands off trying to fix it so He could. I quit worrying and started praying for total restoration with my husband and all those individuals that were involved. Another incident took place when we were at my moms house one night. One of the individuals in my husbands life that had not been speaking to him for months, just unexpectedly called him. I could tell when he walked outside to take the call that something was wrong. When I walked outside to check on him after about 45 minutes, he turned on the speaker on his phone so I could listen to the conversation. This individual was clearly messed up on something and was threating to commit suicide. Even though I had not ever met this individual, I knew what she meant to my husband. So I told him to come on and we would go over there. We did. And when we got there my husband introduced me to her. I told her I was not there to discuss her and my husband's issue, but I was there to talk to her as far as threatening suicide. I just wanted to be a friend she could talk to. I told her I had training in dealing with this issue in my prior recovery training. From the time we got there she was in my face screaming at me, cussing me, cussing him, calling me names and telling me things that I did not even have a clue about. After being there over an hour, I was getting worn out from the drama and hearing her talk down to both of us. I was trying to be very patient with her. I asked her if she minded if I prayed with her, and she turned around and literally spit in my face. At this point I was done. I was not going to continue putting up with her actions towards me or my husband anymore and I certainly did not deserve to be spit on. I left him on the porch with her and I went to wait in the car. This was just another example of me trying to reach out to these people to try and help make things better, but it just didn't work.

Over the course of the next few weeks, I watched my husband sinking into a massive depression and just felt so sorry for him. I knew there was just nothing I could do to fix it. Even in the midst of all this going on with him, we were both still excited to have each other, and he always told me how much he appreciated me sticking by him through all he was going through. We had been married now for four months.

It was on a Wednesday night, and I was coming home from work. I knew my husband had his step-study party at the recovery program he was attending on Thursday night. I was on my way to the grocery store to pick up stuff to bake cookies that night so he would have something to take to the party.

When I got home and walked into the house, the stove was on, and there was a bag of rice that the water had boiled out of, and it was burning. I looked around and noticed the front door was wide open also. I went looking for my husband, and he was in the bedroom on the bed. I asked him what he was doing, why the pot was burning on the stove and why the front door was open.

Right when he spoke, I knew he was messed up. I was so upset because I had never seen him that messed up before. I walked back into the kitchen, and he followed me. I was standing at the pantry. He walked up behind me, then he threw his arms around me and kind of fell into me.

Clearly he was heavily medicated. He said, with very slurred words and barely being able to open his eyes. "Isn't it okay to love on my beautiful wife?"

I turned toward him and said, "What is wrong with you? What have you taken?"

It was right when I said that, he started to scream, "I am so tired of you accusing me of being a drug addict!"

Then he turned around and walked down the hall to the bedroom and sat back on the bed. I walked into the bedroom, and he was furious because I was questioning him as to what medication he had taken and why. He said he got upset earlier in the day at work over an email he had received and that he had taken something when he got home to calm down. He never told me what upset him. We never got that far.

He started to scream, "Can't I get upset? Can't I take something to calm me down without you calling me a drug addict?"

He then took the bottle of medicine and threw it against the closet door. It busted, and pills went everywhere.

I was stunned. I had never seen this in him. I reached down and got my purse and told him I was going to finish some Christmas shopping at the mall. I let him know that I was not going to put up with him cussing and throwing things at me. So I told him that I would be back later when he could calm down.

He said, "Fine, I am going to sleep."

He got his Ambien bottle near the bed, took one, and turned the light off.

It was now around 6:30 p.m. I left so upset So I went to the mall. I did not know what I could do anymore to help him. I was crying and just went and sat on the benches in the mall. While I sat there, watching people walk by, I kept thinking about what in the world was going on with him and what had happened to the person I knew before we got married. It just made me so sad. I stayed until they were closing the mall and knew I had to go back home. I felt he would be good and asleep and we would just talk about it the next day. Then I would figure out what to do about the medication he was taking.

I got home around 9:10 to 9:15 p.m., and when I pulled up to the house, I saw his car was gone. I thought, *What in the world is up with this?* He had never left like that before. Then it started to hit me: *Oh my, he has taken an Ambien.*

I called him time and time again, and he would not answer. Finally, he called back around 9:45 p.m. and was talking crazy about killing himself, and told me he could not take the pain anymore. I told him he had fifteen minutes to get home or I was calling the police. He told me he was coming home and not to call them.

I said, "You are out driving around on Ambien, and you could kill someone. You have fifteen minutes, and I am calling the cops."

It was around 10:30 p.m., and my husband still had not gotten home. I went into his office to see if I could find a tag receipt where he had paid for a tag in order to get the make and year of his car and his license plate number. When I went into the office and sat at his desk, that was when I found the suicide note he had hand written on the back of our checkbook. We had the voucher checks that had three to a page, which made it the size of a regular sheet of paper. He had written it on two pages of checks.

I started to panic and ran into our room to look for his gun on top of the dresser where he kept it. But it was gone. The fear that overcame me was incredible and indescribable. I called our pastor, screaming, and crying. He asked me to read him the note. I did, and he said he was on his way. I then called my best friend, Missy, and her husband, and by that time, it was after 11:00 p.m. Since I did not find a tag receipt, it was then that I called his parents to ask them if they knew the make and year, or tag number of his car.

While I was on the phone with his stepmother, explaining to them what was going on, my husband came walking through the back door. When I saw him, I fell to my knees in the kitchen floor and just hung up on his stepmother. I was screaming, "How could you do this to me, how could you scare me and everyone else this way?!" Then I told him I had called the police and his parents.

Right when I told him I had called the police, he immediately went into the office to get the suicide note. I grabbed the checkbook out of his hand fearing he was going to destroy the note before the police got there. Right at that time, the police pulled up and came in the house and asked him to sit down on the couch. When he sat down, I saw he had grease all over his arms and his hands, as if he had been working on a car. With him having a desk job that was very unusual.

The policeman asked him where he had been, and he said, "Just out riding around." I handed the suicide note to the policeman and told him what had happened. My husband kept telling him, "I have worked for the federal government for twenty-nine years. I get drug tested all the time. She thinks I am on drugs, but I would never do that." He went into the story of the individual in his past that had this problem and why he would never do that.

The officer asked me if he could speak to me in our bedroom, so I followed him back there. He began by saying, "I can tell he is on something because he keeps repeating himself over and over, and I can tell by his behavior, his face being beet red, and he is sweating profusely. He asked me if I knew how much or what he had taken, and I said I did not know. I proceeded to tell him the medication I knew he took for a fact, but I was not for sure of anything else for certain."

He went back out there to talk to my husband and asked him where his gun was. My husband told him it was in his car under the seat and that he never intended to do anything; he was just upset and angry. He told the officer that he had some situations that day at work, and on top of that, he had gotten some e-mails that had really upset him earlier in the day, and he came home and took a nerve pill. The policeman asked him about the Lortab, and my husband said he had only taken two, and two muscle relaxants.

By then, our pastor was coming in, along with Missy and her husband, David. As soon as our pastor got there, the police officer said, "Since your pastor is here, I am going to go ahead and go."

My husband was so worried about his job finding out that I had called the police, he asked the officer to not put anything about the suicide note in his report, because of his job. The officer assured him that he would write it up as a domestic call so it would not go on the record as a suicide attempt. The officer took the note in a ziplock bag and left and asked my pastor to step outside so he could talk to him.

When my pastor came back in, we all sat in the living room, and they all tried to tell my husband he needed to go to the hospital. They kept telling him if he was not on something, then something else was terribly wrong. Everyone in that room—our pastor, his wife, Missy, and David—all knew my husband was on something, and now that everyone had seen it for themselves, he could not deny anymore there was a problem. They stayed at our home until two o'clock in the morning, begging and pleading with him to go to the hospital, to no avail. I knew he was not going to go due to what he had in his system.

My pastor advised me to leave that night and to go home with Missy. They felt it was not safe for me to be there at home with my husband in that condition. I told them all, "He has just threatened suicide. If I was to leave him tonight and he did something to himself, I would never be able to live with it."

So with that, it was getting late, and I had to make a decision. I looked at him, and he had tears in his eyes, and I knew I could not leave him in the shape he was in. I told our pastor and Missy that I was choosing to stay, and that was what I did.

We went to bed, and I turned over and scooted toward the far end of the mattress—you know, what you do when you are mad at each other and you hang on to the edge of the mattress, thinking you're going to hit the floor at any minute. Well, he came to bed, scooted way over against my back, put his hand on my shoulder, and said, "Christie, I am so sorry. I love you more than anything, and I just don't know what to do."

I turned over and put my head on his chest, and I said, "I know you do. Don't worry, sweetie, we will do whatever we need to do to get some help. Don't worry about your job. You are where you can retire, anyway." I proceeded to tell him, "You have to take care of you first. Neither your job nor me is going to matter if you don't get this under control."

I told him I loved him and I would do whatever we needed to do. I was in this, and I was not going to leave him. He was so worn out. I rolled back over to go to sleep. He laid his hand across my neck, on my back and drifted off to sleep, like a scared child, one who had to be touching me. It was so sweet. Even though with all the turmoil that had just happened, that moment was sweet.

By this time, it was already around 3:30 a.m., almost 4:00 a.m. We woke up around 7:00 a.m. He had never been that late going to work, and I knew he had overslept. He did not seem to be too concerned and got in the shower and got ready to leave. I was putting my makeup on, worn out from just a few hours of sleep, and getting ready to go to work. He stood in the doorway for what seemed to be forever, just looking at me, until I said, "Honey, are you okay?"

He said, "Yes, I just want you to know how much I love you."

I said, "I know you do, and I love you too. Try not to worry about all of this today. We will sort it out together and figure out what we need to do. I love you."

He looked at me and smiled, kissed me on my forehead and walked out the door.

As I was leaving for work that beautiful Thursday morning on December 13, I was walking to my car when my phone rang. Again, it was another phone call that was fixing to shatter my world.

The US Marshals proceeded to tell me that my husband had a critical accident and that I needed to get to the University of Alabama at Birmingham Hospital as soon as possible. They told me, "At this point, he is still alive, but you need to get there quickly."

Upon arrival at the hospital, it was as if I was watching a horror movie unfold right before my eyes and I was the main character. When I got into the room, several of the hospital staff were in there and proceeded to tell me that my husband had shot himself in the federal courthouse, where he had been employed for twenty-nine years. Because he did it in a federal courthouse, it was all over the news, and the media was everywhere.

I could not move. I was paralyzed with a gut-wrenching fear that was incredible. The first thing I asked was if the lady he shot himself in front of was okay. That question was prompted by conversations he and I had a few weeks prior to this event. The stress of "year-end" job duties had frustrated him. He would come home and tell me how angry he was at several of his co-workers. He made a comment that night while I was cooking dinner that will stick with me forever. He was talking to me about how much he hated this one particular person that he worked with, and he said,

I guarantee you this, if I ever did commit suicide, I would kill her first and then kill myself.

I hollered at him for even saying such a thing and told him he better not ever say something like that again. I never thought another thing about it, until the day he killed himself. I was so afraid when I was told that he shot himself that he had harmed his coworker also. Thank God he didn't, but I do know that it was only through God's grace that he did not kill her. I know she will always have the memory of seeing him do what he did, and that is bad enough. I just truly thank God that she is alive. I did call the individuals involved at his job to see if I could come speak to them in person, but I was told no. She did not realize just how lucky she was, nor was I ever given the chance to tell her. I knew it was once again by God's grace that while he was standing there for so long in that doorway that morning, that it was the Holy Spirit who prompted me at that moment to tell him it was all going to be okay, and that I loved him. I think that is what made the difference in him walking off and not harming me in the process.

I was in a total state of shock, and my heart was just breaking. I will never forget that doctor walking into the room with my husband's wedding ring around his finger and telling me he had done all he could do.

I just started screaming, "No, no, no!" I was paralyzed with the most unbelievable fear I had ever felt in my life. My heart was not only crushed but also smashed, to the point I felt nothing but numbness for months to come. I felt as if I could not breathe, eat or sleep for quite a while after this happened. There was so much I don't remember in the weeks following his death, due to my total state of shock.

My biggest question to God was why. Why, God, why? I certainly didn't understand after all I had been through in my life. I was so sold out to him, and I was living for him in every way I could, so why did this have to happen to me? All I had ever wanted was for someone to love me unconditionally and to be able to feel some sense of security again. I truly thought that I had found that with my husband. But no, here we go once again. In a matter of minutes, my world was shattered.

Through the days and months afterward, I was still finding myself questioning God and felt my heart starting to harden toward God. That was when God started to sweetly and gently remind me that it was not Him that caused my husband to do this but that my husband had a free will. My husband made the choice to abuse taking his medication, and he also made the choice of what he was going to do that morning in the federal courthouse.

Unfortunately, what people did not know, other than his family and myself, was that this was not my husband's first attempt to commit suicide. His first suicide attempt was five years ago, which had happened way before he ever met me. He was still with his ex-wife at that point. His ex-wife had left something at home that she needed for work and just happened to go home early that day to get whatever it was that she needed.

To me, her going back home early was nothing short of God's grace, because he told me that she never came home early for anything.

When his ex-wife arrived home, she found he was on the bed, unconscious She saw the pill bottle and knew what he had done and called 911. He was taken to Brookwood Medical Center, where they pumped his stomach and then he was put on the psychiatric unit there for a few days.

My husband did share that with me before we married, but remember, I had struggled with that seven years ago myself. So I just assumed that this was in his past, and we all have skeletons from our past. I just figured, like myself, he had already moved past all that. When he was telling me about it before we married, he asked me to please not ever say a word about it because of his job, and if they ever found out, he was afraid he would be fired. I asked him how he got by with not telling them and being off work the time that he was. He told me his ex-wife called them and told them he needed to take his vacation time, and that is what he did, but they never knew the truth as to what had really happened.

It was not until after his death that I learned about all the medication he was actually being prescribed from several different doctors. Every one of the medications he was taking did have suicidal effects. Remember when I said I was asking God why? Well, shortly after my husband's death, God started to reveal to me the reason he had put my husband in my life. God started to unfold to me the realization of what he was up to in all of this, and it was the sweetest moment that I had since my husband's death.

Let me try to explain that a little more. I do know that God knows and sees our future, and he already knows what is going to happen before it ever happens. He is God. He knows it all. He knows what is going to happen in our lives way in advance, even when we don't have a clue. I do believe now and see evidence that God used me as a tool in my husband's life. I just can't help but think that God knew, because of my past, that I was one person strong enough to walk through all of this and make it through it. So now, in the midst of asking why, it all started to make sense, and God started helping me understand.

Just as soon as we started dating, my husband got involved with me at Church, and we were there every Sunday. He had also started a men's step study, which is a year long process, at a local recovery program. He was really working hard on himself and on some of the issues he had from his past. He knew he had a lot he needed to work through. The good news was that he saw it, recognized it, and was willing to do something about it; he wanted to become a better person in all those areas where he felt he was lacking.

He wrote me a letter which was just one of the many ways through his process that I saw God working on him and softening his heart. He continued to meet with Art, who was his sponsor, every week after work.

One night, David came home and said, "Christie, there is something I need to read to you."

I said, "Okay, what is it?"

He pulled out this letter, which was in his handwriting and that I still have, and he started to read it to me. It said,

> *Christie I need to apologize to you for several things I did the last couple of days. First, I apologize for shutting down. More importantly I apologize for insinuating suicide. It was wrong and I know it hurt you. Finally, I apologize for the idle threats regarding divorce. I do love you deeply and I hope at some point you will forgive me.*

This letter he wrote to me was just one of many ways that I saw God working in his life. I thought I would share with you some of his questions and answers out of his step-study book so you can just see how God was working in his life. It reveals how my husband was recognizing his shortcomings and how he was letting God get to the deepest part of him.

1. Question: How can your higher power Jesus Christ help restore you to make sane decisions? How do you get a second chance?

    Answer: This is what I am hoping to get out of this study. More than anything I want to learn now who I am in Christ and who he is in me, like my new wife keeps telling me about. I want to learn that my identity is in him and not in my past dysfunction. I want peace and happiness again, and contentment in my heart. I don't want to have anger or bitterness in my heart anymore. I want to truly be able to get closer to God now more than ever, in every aspect of my life. To have a real love relationship with Him and while growing in relationship with Him, in return it will make me a better husband, father, son, and brother.

2. Question: What areas of your life are out of control, unmanageable? Be specific.

   Answer: My relationships, there are several that need to be made whole again. I have hatred and bitterness in my heart towards several people. I do not want any of this in my life; I know it is not Christ-like. I have a hard time trusting people.

3. Question: How can your relationship with your Higher Power Jesus Christ, help you step out of your denial and face reality?

   Answer: By placing in motion the Scripture that tells us to love others as Christ loved the church and to be slow to anger and quickly to forgive. God is always at work and it is always for my good.

   "Instead, let the Spirit renew your thoughts and attitudes." Ephesians 4:23 (NLT)

4. Question: In what areas of your life are you now ready to let God help you?

   Answer: I am already seeing God teaching me patience. It is not easy especially for someone like me that demands answers and satisfaction now. I have improved though. I am also willing to allow God to help me with anger and bitterness.

5. Questions: What things are you ready to change in your life? Where can you get the power to change them?

   Answer: The power to change comes from the Word, which causes a change in me. Once others see that change in me, I pray for complete restoration in all broken relationships in my life.

6. Question: How have your past expectations of yourself or others been unrealistic?

   Answer: In conversing with people, when I know they do not share the same values and morals that I do, or see things from my point of view. Expecting others to heal from hurts on my time table although they may not be getting help at all.

7. Question: What area of your life are you ready to release control of and hand over to God?

Answer: All areas. This has been a major problem for me in my life. I have harbored bitterness and sometimes even hatred towards others. This is not a Godly way to handle my problems and hurts. I have a problem with immediately reacting instead of processing a Godly solution. I am so striving to improve in this area.

It wasn't until after my husband's death that I learned that he had not been living a close life with the Lord as he had led me to believe prior to us marrying. Or, let me put it this way, the fruit he was bearing, prior to us meeting, were not the fruit of living a Christ-like life. It was after his death I found out that he had struggled with a pornography addiction. I had thought on so many occasions that he was looking at porn, because after we married, the things he would say and do made me question him often about it. I also knew the signs of someone who was into pornography from counseling with others, and being in leadership at recovery.

But every time I asked my husband about it, he would just deny it and say he had never, nor would he ever, look at porn. But after his death, my thoughts were confirmed when I found out that this had been a huge problem in his past. By my observation, he really blamed God for not fixing his family situation, which led to his divorce, and had hardened his heart toward God in many different ways. I know he was carrying a lot of anger and resentment and bitterness toward God and everyone else in his life at the time.

But as he was going through his step study, I started to notice that his heart was really changing. It is so sweet to me now to have his step-study book, which was written in his handwriting. I know beyond a shadow of a doubt that he was chasing Jesus and I do know today that he is sitting right there at the right hand of Christ. I do know the good fruits he was bearing before he died. He was even learning not to lash out at others in the e-mails he received, or to lash out at others anywhere, but to take time to pray before he answered each one. He would send me his e-mails and say, "Okay, honey, is this loving them well?"

That is why I feel so strongly about us meeting. It may have meant the choice between heaven and hell for my husband. Do not misunderstand what I am trying to say. I am not saying it was me that changed my husband. Let me re-iterate strongly: it was not me, but God using me as his tool to help my husband get back where he needed to be in his heart with Jesus. It was only God that was slowly but surely changing my husband's heart, and I got to be a part of seeing God work in his life.

The one thing I do know is that my husband did not have near the anger, hate and bitterness in his heart when he died, that he had when I met him. He was learning to take responsibility for his actions and started forgiving others that had hurt him. I am very thankful to have been a part of his journey the last six months of his life, and I know, beyond a shadow of a doubt, that he was so hungry for Christ. And I do know where he is today.

One other thing I really pray about now is that God will work a miracle of restoration with me and all those individuals involved. That is all my husband ever wanted, and I pray one day for his sake that God will make that happen. I don't want his death to be in vain, I would love to see that what Satan meant for evil, for God to turn it around and use it for His good. So agree with me, if you will that it will happen.

Here is just another incident of how God so sweetly worked in this situation. You judge for yourself: coincidence or God's grace?

I had shared my testimony at recovery several years ago. One of the ladies that had come that night heard my testimony and came up to me afterward. She wanted to know if I would sponsor her if she went through a step study. I told her I would pray about it and would let her know. We both prayed about it, and then I told her I would.

She had just begun her year long step study, and that was when we started our journey together. I will never forget the first time we met, and she started to share with me about her husband who had committed suicide. I was astounded. I had never dealt with a suicide situation at this point, nor did I know anyone who had. She started opening up to me and sharing her feelings about how her husband's suicide had affected her. She was sharing her feelings with me. She felt she was not woman enough for him to live for. She had feelings that she wasn't a good wife, questioning what she could have done differently and feeling so alone and abandoned. I mean, her feelings from this were all over the board from guilt, shame, abandonment, inadequacy, self-esteem—just a whole lot of issues.

I remembered the first time we met. We talked in great length about her childhood through adulthood and about the suicide of her husband. We talked about how we were going to work throughout the year and have her start to deal with and process through each one of these issues, and to show her how God could, and would, restore her. I told her I would help throughout the year in guiding her through his Word so she did not have to carry these feelings anymore, because he was carrying them for her. I never knew two years later she would be sharing these same words with me and that I would have to remember all the counsel that I had given her. I remembered everything I had ever told her play by play, and now it was my turn to walk through all the feelings that she had dealt with.

It was sweet to see how God put Peggy in my life when He did. She was there the day my husband shot himself, comforting me and talking to me and knowing the exact pain I was feeling that day. When my home was full of people that day and they would say, "I am so sorry. I cannot imagine what you are going through," I knew that if you had not actually experienced something like that yourself, it is so true, that you just can't know. But see, she did understand because she had walked through it herself. She knew exactly how to pray for me every day, through all of the situations and feelings I was having, and going to have in the weeks to come. To this day, I am still her sponsor, and we continue to meet every week. She doesn't realize that she helps me more than I help her, every time we get together.

Yes, she processed through all her stuff, and you would not believe that she is the same woman I met a few years ago. Yes, she still struggles with life's problems day to day, as we all do, but now she knows to go straight to His Word to get her answers as to how to handle a situation in a healthy Godly way—His way. This year, she started leading a step study at recovery for yet another group of women; yes, this same woman who told me two years ago she could never do what I do.

Guess what? When she thought she couldn't, God assured her she could. This was no coincidence, sweet friends. This was a grand overall picture of God's grace and how He works. This is why I continuously talk about us living by example and making others want what it is we have. We need to be contagious so that others that cross our paths will see a walking picture in us of God's grace. You know, you may be the only Jesus they will ever see.

1 Thessalonians 3:12 (NLT)

12 And may the Lord make your love for one another and for all people grow and overflow, just as our love for you overflows.

If we are full of God's love, it will overflow to others. It's not enough merely to be courteous to others; we must actively and persistently show love to them. Our love should be growing continually. If your capacity to love has remained unchanged for some time, ask God to fill you again with his never-ending supply. Then look for opportunities to let his love spill over in refreshment to others.

Think about that for a minute. Do you get angry or agitated at someone quickly instead of extending grace and loving them well? Are you rude or critical to others? Or how about when going to a restaurant and your waiter or waitresses are not waiting on you as quickly as you think they should? Do you show them grace, or are you short and rude? Think about when you're at work and how you deal with your co-workers. Or how about when you're on the interstate and another driver, for one reason or another, does something to make you angry?

Just take a minute to reflect on what you do on a daily basis, wherever you go, whoever you come in contact with every day.

Reflect on 1 Thessalonian 3:12 (NLT)

> *[12] And may the Lord make your love for one another and for all people grow and overflow, just as our love for you overflows. pray first and then answer these questions.*

Questions:

1. Are you a contagious Christian? If I were to meet you, would I want what you have?

2. Do you treat your family in your home the same as outside your home?

3. Do you act the same way outside from church, as you act inside church?

4. Start looking at yourself in all situations, and answer this question: are you loving well and giving others grace?

5. List some changes you could make in your life to love others better and put into action the fruits of the spirit? Galatians 5:22-23 (NLT) 22 But the Holy Spirit produces this kind of fruit in our lives: love, joy, peace, patience, kindness, goodness, faithfulness, 23 gentleness, and self-control. There is no law against these things!

6. List some of your character traits that you could work on to get better in these areas?

7. List some people in your life that you could love better and extend some grace to?

Colossians 2:20–23 in the NLT *Life Application Study Bible*:

People should be able to see the difference between the way Christians and non-Christians live. Still, we should not expect instant maturity in new Christians. Christian growth is a lifelong process. Although we have a new nature, we don't automatically think all good thoughts and have all pure attitudes when we become new people in Christ. But if we keep listening to God, we will be changing all the time.

As you read Colossians 2:20-23 ask yourself this question.

Question:

1. As you look over your past, list what changes for the better you have seen in your thoughts and attitudes. Change may be slow, but your life will change significantly if you trust God to change you.

Colossians 1:8 in the NLT *Life Application Study Bible:*
Because of their love for one another, Christians can have an impact that goes far beyond their neighborhoods and communities. Christian love comes from the Holy Spirit.

After reading colossians 1:8 answer these questions.

1. What are some "thoughts" and "attitudes" you still have that you would like to see changed?

2. What will be your plan to put good in, so good can come out where these areas will start to change?

Example: If you have a bad attitude at work for whatever reason, or you work with a not-so-easy-to-get-along-with co-worker, how can you make a plan to change that? Maybe listen to praise music on the way to work and start thanking Him for your job by praying gratitude, no matter how bad it is, and ask Him to change your attitude on your job. As Christians we have to continuously realize that we may be the only

Jesus people ever see. Now with the co-worker go out of your way to do something kind or to say something kind throughout the day (to make a conscious effort). You never know what is going on in others lives as to why they act like they do. So it is very important that you come up with some sort of plan. Look up Scripture on your thoughts and attitudes. Put them in your purse or in your car or in your wallet. When you start to struggle with that particular thought or attitude you will have God's Word to handle it in a more Godly way. For example, if you are feeling frustrated at work quote:

Isaiah 41:10 Fear not, for I am with you; be not dismayed, for I am your God; I will strengthen you, I will help you, I will uphold you with my righteous right hand.

You can google anything these days. If you are dealing with fear, just Google "Scripture on fear", etc. I have even googled scriptures on loneliness after I lost my husband. And being single again, I cling to those every day.

1 Tim 5:5 in the (NLT) "The widow who is really in need and left all alone puts her hope in God and continues night and day to pray and to ask God for help."

You see, even in the thicket of losing my husband, I had people come up to me and say, "How come every time I see you, knowing what you have just been through, you're still smiling? How can you be so bubbly and happy?"

I tell them why: I was sitting on my bed one morning, feeling so hopeless, and there were days I would not even get out of bed. But that morning, something was different. I felt the presence of God so strongly. It felt as if God was sitting right there on my bed. I was looking out the window when he so sweetly laid this Scripture on my heart and gently reminded me.

1 Peter 1:6–7 in the NLT *Life Application Study Bible*:

We must accept trials as part of the refining process that burns away impurities and prepares us to meet Christ. As gold is heated, impurities float to the top and can be skimmed off. Likewise, our trials, struggles and persecutions refine and strengthen our faith, making us useful to God. Instead of asking, "Why me?" we should respond to suffering with a new set of responses:

1. Confidence that God knows, plans and directs our lives for the good. It's hard to calculate sometimes, but God always provides his love and strength for us. God leads us toward a better future.
2. Perseverance when facing grief, anger, sorrow and pain. We express our grief, but we don't give in to bitterness and despair.
3. Courage because with Jesus as brother and Savior, we need not be afraid. He who suffered

for us will not abandon us. Jesus carries us through everything.

This is what the Lord started laying on my heart that morning:

Christie, are you still going to love Me now, are you still going to trust Me now, as you go through this most difficult situation, believing yourself, as to what you have been telling others about Me?

And this is what I was telling others:

Listen, no situation is hopeless. If you're still breathing, there is hope. And hope does know your name. That God has a plan and a hope for your future, and ALL things work together for the good to those that love Christ".

In Romans 8:28 (nlt) and we know that God causes everything to work together for His good to those who love God and are called according to His purpose for them.

He doesn't say "SOME" things He says "ALL" things. So once again back to that same question,

Christie are you going to believe this for yourself this morning, or are you going to let the enemy steal kill and destroy you, which is exactly what he wants to do? Either My promises in My Word are true or they are not. Either you believe it or you don't. Can you praise Me in this storm? I am the same God Christie, that promises that I will not put anything more on you than you can handle.

And with that, I just started to cry. That morning, I said, "Yes, God, I do believe what I have been sharing with others, and yes, I will believe it right now for myself."

That day, I made a choice. I chose to be happy and not be down. I chose to get up and say, "This is the day the Lord has made, and I will rejoice and be glad in it." I started doing that everyday, whether I felt like it or not. There were times I did not want to get out of bed, and when I did, I tried to put on my makeup to go to work, but it was off from me crying by the time I got to the car. But the main thing is, I got to the car, and I kept going even when I did not feel like it. It was not on my own strength but with His strength, knowing that sometimes we just don't understand other people, nor do we understand why they do what they do. The reality is that we all have free will, so why is it then, when anything goes wrong in our lives, we want to blame God?

The truth is, most of the time, we make our own decisions in life without even consulting God. We just make the decision on our own, and then we end up blaming God for the outcome. I think we have to remember that God created a perfect world, but when

Adam and Eve went against what He wanted, that led to this sinful world, which created our sinful nature. Consequences of their sin then created every outcome of struggles, situations, circumstances, disease, cancer or just whatever is negative that you have to deal with in your life. Boy, am I going to have a bone to pick with Adam and Eve when I get up there. LOL

Sometimes we wonder why our lives go the way they do, and we always seem to ask the question or wonder, "Why, God, why?" It could be things you had control over or things you had absolutely no control over. We have to deal with it anyway, just like the one I found myself in with my husband's suicide.

As I continued to pray and ask God, "Where are you now?" I almost felt as if God was being silent and not hearing my prayers. Then I started doing a Bible study shortly after my husband's death, and started getting in the Word every day. Because I had to do my homework on the Bible study. It was then that God started showing me His answers through His Word. You see, He speaks to us through his Word. If you just pick one Scripture a day and ask Him to show you something about that Scripture, He will. This is the kind of relationship He so longs for with you. Through His Word is where I started to look for understanding in what was going on in my life.

If you look at Lazarus's story in John 11:1–45, you will see where he felt just like I did. You will see where Martha told Jesus, "If you would have been here, my brother would not have died." I think what Jesus was showing her was that if He would have healed Lazarus or showed up when she thought He should have, she would have missed coming to understand Jesus in a much deeper way. Martha knew Jesus could have healed her brother, because she had seen Him do it before. But Jesus wanted her to walk through the process to move her in a closer relationship to Him and to help her learn to trust Him.

Another good example from the Bible involves David's life. Pastor Matthew taught this one Sunday. It was so good, I have to share it:

1 Samuel 16–17 in the NLT *Life Application Study Bible*:
When we think of David, we think of the following: shepherd, poet, giant-killer, king, ancestor of Jesus—in short, one of the greatest men in the Old Testament. But alongside that list stands another: betrayer, liar, adulterer and murderer. The first list gives qualities we all might like to have. The second, qualities that might be true of any one of us. The Bible makes no effort to hide David's failures. Yet he is remembered and respected for his heart for God. Knowing how much more we share in David's failures than in his greatness, we should be curious to find out what made God refer to David as a man after His own heart (Acts 13:22).

David, more than anything else, had an unchangeable belief in the faithful and forgiving nature of God. He was a man who lived with great zest. He sinned, but he was quick to confess his sins. His confessions were from the heart, and his repentance was genuine. David never took God's forgiveness lightly or His blessing for granted. God never held back from David either His forgiveness or the consequences of David's actions. David experienced the joy of forgiveness even when he had to suffer the consequences of his sins.

We tend to get these two reversed. Too often we would rather avoid the consequences than experience forgiveness. Another big difference between us and David is that while he sinned greatly, he did not sin repeatedly. He learned from his mistakes because he accepted the suffering they brought. Often we don't seem to learn from our mistakes or the consequences that result from those mistakes.

List some changes it would take for God to find this kind of obedience in you? _____
_____
_____

Here were the lessons from David's life:

1. His willingness to honestly admit his mistakes was the first step in dealing with them.
2. His forgiveness did not remove the consequences of sin.
3. He realized that God greatly desires our complete trust and worship.

You can continue reading his story from 1 Samuel 16 to 1 Kings 2.

In chapter 17: it really shows us how to become a champion. Here is what that looks like:

1. A champion stands up where others pull back.
2. A champion shows others they can do what God is calling them to do.
3. A champion is not devoid of fear; they are filled with purpose. Even though you may feel fear sometimes, it does not mean you are not a champion.
4. A champion sees the purpose.
5. A champion will not use the weapons of the enemy, such as doing to others what they have done to us in order to pay them back.
6. A champion will let go of whatever they are holding on to when God is telling them to let it go and put it down.
7. A champion inspires other champions.

Sometimes it is through our struggles that Jesus wants us to know Him in a much bigger revelation than we could ever understand. Just because He is not answering us when we think He should, does not mean He is rejecting us. It means He is working on something so much greater for us that we just can't see at the moment. Sometimes he is bringing us to a place in our circumstances to make us totally dependent on Him. So once again, it is our choice. Are we going to seek Him and ask Him to help us understand and to show us from His perspective why we are in a particular situation? Or are we going to let that circumstance destroy us and look at it in the middle of our problem and see no way out, like my husband did?

I made the choice to adjust my life to understand what Jesus was doing, and to join Him there. I knew when I responded to Him in this way. He would help me to know Him at a much deeper level. When you are sitting and asking yourself, "Why is this happening to me?" think about Job and all he went through.

Read Job chapters 1 and 2. Everything he owned was destroyed, his children were killed and he had excruciating sores all over his body. I am sure Job was asking God the same question we are: why? I know he, for sure, did not know how his story would end, but he was a great example of not looking at his situation from the middle of all his mess. He was looking for God's perspective in it all.

If we continue to look at our mess while we are in the middle of it, we will have a distorted view of God and start to think He is a cruel God who does not love us due to our own our circumstance. And that, my friend, is the furthest thing from the truth. We need to start looking at our circumstances from the heart of God, get in His Word, and ask Him to help us understand and show us an answer through His word.

We need to consider our circumstances, and give God the glory for how He got us out of it, and then allow Him to use it. In return, we can help others grow in a relationship with Him by our experiences.

I just continue each day to hang on to His promises. Sometimes it is minute by minute, hour by hour, day by day, week by week month by month. But every day I've grown stronger. We just have to continue to realize He is still working behind the scenes even when we are not seeing it. We must realize that He is still on the throne.

But God is the One that does know what is going on in each of our lives and in each of our situations. He just so sweetly reminds us that when we continue to keep our focus on a Big "God," our problems will start looking "smaller." In other words, when we maximize God, it will minimize our struggle.

There are still times that come up now that I don't understand, or I have people who hurt me whom I need to forgive and let off the hook. I try to remember that when I choose to forgive them for hurting me. God sweetly reminds me that I will be the one set free. Sometimes we just need to stop and evaluate where we are with these problems and individuals that we're struggling with. We need to let go and turn them over to God and let Him have His way and will in it, and then sit back and rest, knowing that once we let go, He will come through at the right time.

God is always on time every time, but we need to continue to pray that we will be on His agenda and not ours. He did have something for me on His agenda the day my husband shot himself. Let me just tell you how God used that enormous hurt that day for his good. Remember me saying earlier in my book that my relationship with my son and my daughter had been estranged? Let me just tell you, for the last seven years, there was no way to try and explain how many people had continued to pray that those relationships with me and my children would be restored. Remember when I said just because I was a Christian now did not instantly fix things with them or make it okay? They had to process through their anger with me the best way they knew how, and in their timing, not mine. And I had to realize it was not going to be in my timing that this healing would happen but in God's timing, and only when my children were ready to forgive me.

I remembered my sponsor telling me, "Christie, you are going to have to be okay with where you are in the Lord and continue to trust in Him, even if your children never forgive you." After that, I never had any unrealistic expectations, and I tried not to get my hopes up that these relationships would ever be fixed. I just trusted God that if I would be patient and wait for His timing and His agenda, not mine, then maybe one day it would happen. The one thing I did know then was that if it did get fixed, it would totally be a God thing and He would get *all* the glory for it.

Well, you probably guessed it; the day my husband died, those prayers were answered. My daughter was there when I drove up from leaving the hospital, and my son got there shortly thereafter. My son asked me if he could talk to me for a minute, and we went back to my room. He and I just sat on my bed, and we cried together and told each other how sorry we both were for hurting each other like we had. My daughter and I had already had this talk last year, and we had worked through more of our stuff at this point than my son and I had.

The three of us were all together as a family for the first time in years, and yes, it was totally a God thing.

He showed up at one of the worst times of my life. It was the sweetest moment, seeing God bring us together in the way that He did and to see that total restoration happen that day. I would have never guessed that one.

It just goes to show you that God can take something so awful, and use it for good. The first thing you need to do is to admit how painful the situation was, or still is, if you are still going through it. Second, while you are persevering through your particular situation acknowledge the negative emotion that it really has caused you, or still may be causing you. Third, you need to try and find something positive, just one little thing in the situation, which in return will give you some sort of hope. While you are walking through your trial, try to see how God is growing you in character, and recognize what you have learned while going through it. Think of your hardship as a pathway to peace.

I would like to encourage you to look up Romans 5:3-5, then answer the following questions.

Romans 5:3-5 (NIV)

3 Not only so, but we also glory in our sufferings, because we know that suffering produces perseverance; 4 perseverance, character; and character, hope. 5 And hope does not put us to shame, because God's love has been poured out into our hearts through the Holy Spirit, who has been given to us.

Question:

1. Do you think whatever it is you are struggling with, or whatever situation you are going through, you could rejoice and be happy in the middle of that situation?

2. While walking through this trial, list some of the ways that you are seeing how God is growing you through this trial. _____
   _____
   _____
   _____

3. List some things you are going through: your struggles, your trial, your hurt, or whatever your suffering may look like in your current situation. _____
   _____
   _____
   _____

4. Now try to list one small, positive thing that you can try to see in each of the things you listed in question 3. _____
   _____
   _____
   _____

5. Then list the things that you feel you might be able to start doing to self help yourself, to help you to get past this situation.

6. List what kind of character traits you feel your particular struggle may be causing you to grow in.

I want you to take an imaginary journey with me for just a minute. Imagine with me, as if you were walking by your coffee table where you had your favorite glass vase sitting—not just any glass vase but a very expensive special vase, one of those that are rare and one of a kind. It was your most favorite piece that you owned in your whole house. And then one day, you were cleaning the coffee table and accidentally knocked it over. You tried as hard as you could to catch it, but it fell onto the hardwood floor and broke into a million pieces.

Now in your mind, picture all those broken pieces all over the floor. It was just a mess. You were so upset because the vase was one of a kind. Because of the glass being so precious, you reached down and picked it up piece by piece, holding each piece in your hand until you had it all gathered. Knowing how special the glass was, you were going to take it to a glass maker to see if he could at least melt down the glass and try to make something else out of it.

So the glass maker does just that. He decides to use a mold that was in the shape of an angel. He puts the broken glass in, piece by piece, and melts it down. He then takes the melted glass and pours it into the mold. He calls you and tells you it is ready. So you go and pick it up.

As the glass maker is walking up to the counter with it, you stand in amazement once you see that it is the most beautiful glass angel you have ever seen in your life. You just stand there looking at it and realize, wow, it's *whole* again, and it's beautiful. How could someone take something that was so broken and make it this whole? The angel you picked up was even more beautiful than the glass vase, and remember, you thought that vase was something special before it broke.

There is so much truth to that story because it is a true example of my real life and of what God did in my life. He took all my brokenness throughout my life, and with every hardship and every struggle He took it piece by piece, and made me whole and beautiful again. Now each time I am faced with a trial, I ask myself, "Am I just trying to find a way to get out of this trial, or instead, am I going to walk through it and get what God wants me to get out of the trial?"

Remember this: when we have the resources at our fingertips to get us out of our trial (taking the easy way out), we miss the work of what God is trying to teach us. We can also miss what He is working on behind the scenes. Walking through a trial the hard way builds character and helps us to grow in Christ and learn who we are in Him in the process. God has never let any of my hurts go unused, and he won't let any of yours either.

First and foremost, I do not want you to feel sorry for me. I want you to look at me and be in awe at what God has done in my life. When you look at me, I want you to truly see this story is all about Him. I have seen God's hand firsthand in my life, and I just try to remember that if I respond to any and all of the circumstances in my life with affirmations of trust, then I am continuing to participate in the process.

Colossians 1:6 in the NLT *Life Application Study Bible*: God's Word is not just for our information; it is for our *transformation*!

Becoming a Christian means beginning a whole new relationship with God, not just turning over a new leaf or determining to do right. New believers have a changed purpose, direction, attitude, and behavior. They are no longer seeking to serve themselves, but they are bearing fruit for God.

How is the good news reaching others through your life?

God doesn't want to leave us the way He found us.

He is saying will you go My way and not miss what all I have for you?

You see, everyone has a book in them. Everyone has a story. The question is, how are you going to use yours? Your story may not be as drastic as others, or mine, but you still have a story that you could be sharing with others. It will help you to take your mind off your own problems, when you're sinking your life into others and loving them well. I look forward to reading your story one day also. Don't let it go to waste. Let God take your hurts and use them for his good. The peace you are searching for is not the absence of something; it is the absence of someone—Jesus.

Philippians 3:12–14 (MSG)
I'm not saying that I have this all together, or that I have it made. But I am well on my way, reaching out for Christ, who has so wondrously reached out for me. Friends, don't get me wrong. By no means do I count myself an expert in all of this, but I've got my eye on the goal, where God is beckoning me onward—to Jesus. I'm off and running, and I'm not turning back, knowing that He is the author of my life, and I will neither doubt nor limit God as to what He can and will do.

I will close my book with this, which is my life verse: "I say this because I know the plans that I have for you" (Jeremiah 29:11, ESV). This message is from the Lord: "I have good plans for you. I don't plan to hurt you. I plan to give you hope and a good future."

Having hope means you need to make a goal, then you need to make a plan, and believe that you will achieve it. When you are hopeful, you will be able to maintain that goal even when you have a difficult situation, or you experience a setback. You need to believe in yourself, that you will adapt to whatever situation you are walking through.

Read Jeremiah 29:11 and answer the following questions

Question:

1. Do you believe He has a good future planned for you?

2. Now do you truly trust He is the author of your life and has your best interest at heart? And are you going to trust him?

3. If He doesn't give you exactly what you are asking, are you still gonna find hope and joy, and know that no matter what the outcome of your situation, realize there is still hope?

4. List a circumstance in your life where hoping and keeping a postive attitude was helpful to you. _____
   _____
   _____
   _____

5. List something positive that came out of a bad experience that was difficult for you to walk through. _____

6. List the situations you are ready to let go and let God. No matter what it is you are going to let them go, and let Him have His way. _____

7. List ways that you can continue to look for hope even in the challenges and difficulties that you are currently experiencing. _____

I really want you to grasp this and really believe this in your heart. Know that He is madly in love with you. You are completely forgiven, fully pleasing, totally accepted, and complete in Him, as stated in John 3:16 (MSG).

16-18 "This is how much God loved the world: He gave his Son, His one and only Son. And this is why: so that no one needs to be destroyed; by believing in Him, anyone can have a whole and lasting life. God didn't go to all the trouble of sending His Son to point an accusing finger, telling the world how bad it was. He came to help, to put the world right again. Anyone who trusts in Him is acquitted; anyone who refuses to trust Him has long since been under the death sentence without knowing it. And why? Because of that person's failure to believe in the one-of-a-kind Son of God when introduced to Him.

I would like to challenge you to continue to write in your journal every day at least three positive things a day that you experienced within the day.

- It can be that someone may have said something kind to you, or you may have said something kind to someone else.

- It could be something that you did fun throughout your day; you may have received some good news, or the Lord showed up for you in a mighty way somehow.

- You may have read something somewhere that really lifted you up or touched you in a profound way. Maybe it was just getting up that morning.

- You can also journal about a particular area that you struggle with; like self-esteem.

- So come up with three things you did during the day that made you proud of yourself.

- Or maybe you are struggling with a spouse or a parent or just someone involved in your life. In some way look for at least three things in that person that were positive that day.

- Or maybe you are just trying spiritually to grow in the Lord. Look for three ways that He helped you to do that. Whatever it is, journal three positive things a day and this will help you to start training your mind to do some positive thinking.

In closing, soak in these scriptures. They are so powerful.

Romans 5:19

By man's disobedience many were made sinners, but by one man's obedience many will be made righteous.

He is saying here we have all in some shape or form shown disobedience which has caused us all to sin. We have all messed up due to our sins. But because Jesus was obedient to His Father that day to die on that cross, we don't have to feel any more guilt or shame. He took that for us the day He died

Thank you Jesus for your obedience. Help us to be just as obedient in our walk with You.

Memorize this verse, Psalm 71:20, and carry it with you daily in your heart, soul and mind.

Psalm 71:20 (MSG) says He can and will restore you.

I finally realize there is no situation that is hopeless, no matter how bad it may seem.

Always remember if you are still breathing, Hope Knows Your Name.

In Memory of
Mindy M. Davis
March 23, 1964 - May 31, 1979

Voices of the Survivors at the Girls Home in

Deidre
Anchorage, Alaska

> I am 41. I was in Indianapolis from the age of 14 to 16.5. Before I went in I was a Christian that had never done drugs or been on a date. I didn't smoke etc. My mother, who had paid someone to take care of me for years didn't want me back. The lady was no longer able to take care of me. I was supposed to graduate the program after the first year, but a week before graduation they pulled me into the office and demoted me saying I didn't raise my hands in church and they felt I had lust in my heart. I was made to go to churches almost every weekend to "give my testimony" where I was the one behind the pulpit to raise funds. They even sent my picture out in flyers and such.
>
> I was definitely exploited for their financial gains. I also remember scrubbing the mess hall floor with my tooth brush all night when I first arrived. I was beaten with a board for telling one

of the counselors that I was afraid of one of the girls that were making advances on me. I was told I should be ashamed of myself for thinking someone was gay that just wanted my love. That is until the night they caught her trying to rape me with a knife and kicked her out. Did they apologize for beating me for trying to come to them for help? No! After leaving, I never set foot in a church again.

I had gone 3 times a week before going to that place. I choose now to have my own relationship with God and not be told I need to raise my hands, speak in tongues, or be slain in the spirit! I am 41 and still remember how I suffered in their hands. I would never send a child there. I now have two adult daughters now and two small step children.

Bonnie
Oklahoma City, Oklahoma

Hi. I was serving time in Indianapolis during 1973 and 1974. I remember that they would take me to the basement for their so-called correction of my attitude. This consisted of me being beaten with their wooden paddle to the point I could hardly sit. This went on every week for the first two months I was there.

Then one night, they took me out of my bed at midnight, to go downstairs and re-wash all the dishes from supper that night. The water was so hot it turned my hands beet red. I told them that it was too hot so they made me bend over the table and gave me 50 swats for my complaining.

The abuse was not necessary. I also remember having severe pain from my stomach and they would not give me anything for it. It was terrible. I can still remember the spankings, the beatings and the pain of being there. Thank God my parents finally came and picked me up.

Kathleen
St. Louis, Missouri

You were not the only one; they had a girl die in Indy before I got there. The director and one of the counselors were charged with abuse when I was there. I lived it and saw it happen to others. If someone was fortunate enough to have a good experience, great, but I have suffered from the trauma for the past 30 years from what happened to me.

I was in Indianapolis in 79 and 80 and had the same horrible experiences there. I was also drug free. But my mother thought I was being controlled by Satan and this would fix me. The director there was charged with abuse, along with a counselor there. The abuse I witnessed was horrendous. We were imprisoned there and not allowed to leave unless our parents wanted to take us out. The facility was barricaded with fence and barbed wire. How people can claim it was not imprisonment beats me.

Terrie
Orlando, Florida

To all my sisters who were there in 1979–1980 I too was at this horrid place…Does anyone remember the closet? This program was a horrid way to hurt and exploit children. If God knew what happened to us, those two directors would have surely been sent to hell…Maybe with any luck…that is what will happen.

Kay
United States

I came back for a stopover, on my way home, the new building, was facing Delaware street, so I went upstairs, using the far left stairway, to my left was a utility closet, I heard voices, I said who is in there, several voices answered, they asked me to let them out, I was still in the program brainwashed mode, so I did not let them out, I was up there later when a staff opened the door, the girls were all sweaty, and in nightgowns, they actually showed me how they figured out how to all fit in there. All these years later and after having 2 kids, I never mistreated my children and its haunting, to believe I could see this, and do nothing. But I can say this, there was some sort of brainwashing going on, I became a staff member, if that is what one would call a person with no training, education, in helping young people, then I have to live with memories, of watching people in the basement, and whatever other chores. They used me to help torment these kids. I tried not to think about this place for years. I have never discussed all that went on with my husband, children or siblings.

Donna 1978
Greenwood, Indiana

> I was around back then. Not a resident, although I did visit the facility. I can confirm that the director did indeed use the kids for her own financial gain. It made the newspapers at the time. If you check the Indianapolis Star newspaper of the period you will find several articles about it there. How do I remember so well? Kids used to come down and clean up the beauty shop where I worked. The director had purchased it and you kids cleaned it. I won't go into any more details, but your report is entirely consistent with what I observed back then.

Tamme
Kansas City, Missouri

> I was in that same program and as a matter of fact I was with Mindy when she died. They made me and another girl Christie, give her salt water to throw up the pills she took…I was thirteen years old. I have never recovered from that event. I ran away after the police questioned me. The staff hadn't even called my parents to tell them what I had gone through. I endured so much abuse there. I still have nightmares about being in the hole of the old house in the laundry room. I was in the corner between two

file cabinets for six weeks. Rats would come in at night...it was horrible. I would like to reach out to the ones that were with me during this period. Nothing good came out of my experience but painful memories of abuse. That director still appears in my dreams flipping the switchblade with her long nails...scary.

Frightened
Westfield, Indiana

The director and her thugs are absolutely the most frightening people I have ever been around. I can't stand to be within 50 feet of either one of them. Someday, I am afraid they will find bodies in the basement of the Third Phase Mansion and it will be the story to end all stories! It will be one for the record books... Bet you'.

Joyce—1
Springfield, Missouri

I also was in this program for several months in 1976. I kept notes in my socks about the abuse there, because they would "raid" our rooms when we would be in bathroom, etc.... They would take us on an outing, or hide us in the basement when the health dept came for inspections—there were far too many occupants for the Fire Codes! I was a little older than most of the others—my psychiatrist had put me on the adult psychiatric unit there in Indianapolis. I got out, then he wanted to put me back in, so my parents wanted me at this particular program instead. My Dad had been a pastor and he and the Indiana church he pastored would have the director come and speak about every year, bringing her entourage of "trophy testimonies" to give their speeches. Mom and Dad didn't believe my reports of abuse there during their visits to me. I wanted to expose the two directors, but did not have the support I needed at that time. I was in college by the time they were arrested in 1980, and then my folks believed me!! (Don't know what I did with those notes). Not every program has these abuse issues—but this one did because of the 2 "hypocrites" that ran it—God will surely judge them for all the abuse I personally witnessed when I was there! I'm glad someone had the backbone to 'blow the whistle'—I only wish it had been me, because I know the abuse continued even after I left up until they were arrested.

Cari

I don't really care about what anyone else thinks or what the media thinks. I was a victim yes a victim of this program in Indianapolis, Indiana. The 2 people who ran it received charges of child abuse and kidnapping. I was there in 1980. I have horrific nightmares and really to this day do not know what happened to these 2 women. But I pray to God, yes to God, they received the punishment that is fit in God's eyes and his will. Horrible!!!!!! Yes victim is the correct word!!! I was wondering if anyone from the Indianapolis, Indiana program was ever put in a closet, it was a Broom closet. If you talked to a new person that came in you were punished I was put into a broom closet about 5x5 with about 4-5 other girls. I really don't see how this helped me to stop trying drugs or running away from home. When I was there, there was no counseling for drugs or for the problems a teenager faces. I am 43 years old now and this to this very day it still haunts me. I am a well-adjusted adult, work full time and have great friends and family. My parents put me in this particular center and I do not blame them. I was a crazy teenager. I thought this would help me. It did not. I finally was taken to the local hospital because I was so upset I started crying and couldn't stop so I started hyper ventilating and couldn't breathe. I told the doctor that examined me about what was going on there at the Indianapolis, Indiana program and that is when they took the director (called mom) to jail and I have all this written down in my old Bible. I was told they received kidnapping and child abuse charges. It does feel so good to finally have the internet to get this all out. It was twenty six years ago and I finally found this forum online. I pray that they were prosecuted I still to this day do not know what has happened to these two women, but pray to God that he had his will and they were dealt with properly. You don't cram the Lord down someone's throat, especially a teenager that needs love and attention and help. We went to church 2 times a day, we cleaned bathroom floors and toilets we did go to a private in-house school. Ok that is it, had to get all that out.

Kathleen
St. Louis, Missouri

I was at the Indianapolis facility in 79 and 80 and both suffered and watched other girls suffer horrible abuse at the hands of the director and counselors. Imprisoning girls against their will and forcing God down someone's throat is not the right way. Jesus would never have done such a thing. There are plenty of things that happen out there that get covered up.

Thirty years later I still suffer from the horrible effects of the mental and physical abuse the young women suffered. I was committed on my thirteenth birthday, not from a drug problem either. I watched horrendous things happen there and for anyone to down play the emotional trauma some people suffered is just crazy. If someone was lucky enough to have had a great experience there, then that is awesome. Not everyone was so lucky. Some parents sent their kids there to force them to embrace God, at any expense, and that is why some call it brainwashing. We would get punished for not saying prayers and singing hymns, etc.…They used items to beat us with and locked us in dark closets and we had to pee in buckets if we were locked in. What young person deserves to be treated like that?

Cricket (nickname)
Detroit, Michigan

I was a victim there as well. I was in the boys house...I left about three days after a girl named Mindy died. They did not call EMS, they just prayed over her and she died. She was fourteen. I suffer from post-traumatic disorder...One of the male directors was the one who locked us in the basement and all we got to eat were bags of left over doughnuts. I was severely underweight. Well I remember them driving us to churches in speedway Indiana and the boys and me would talk about food the way most boys talk about sex or sports or cards...we might get two eggs once a month...we would brush our teeth with old amway toothpaste. The tubes were made of lead and it stained some kids teeth...I woke up last week screaming because I dreamed I was locked in the basement again...I was frozen with fear...I was there in 1978 through 1981. I was in the boys house where we were the forgotten ones. I remember everything from locking the windows, doors; even the refrigerator was locked with seat belts. There was feces floating in the shower in the basement, and we never got enough to eat. Sometimes our dinner was popcorn and the director would pimp us out at church meetings and would get them to give her money. Even with her making all her money, I knew that all we would have for dinner would be doughnuts. I was so underweight. I have had such vivid nightmares of being locked in that basement with one day bleeding into the next. I wanted to think the girls had it a little better, but now I see you all were living in your own hell. I felt no love, and I will never forget the girl named Mindy that I believe they let die. She was so young and so nice to me. I wonder why they were never charged with murder?

Elizabeth-Nancy
Las Vegas, Nevada

After scrolling through all the comments, I was astonished to read so many similar accounts of the experience I had during the two and a half years at the same Indianapolis program (I believe it was around 1972–1975 or during 1973–1976). Precious teenage years were squandered living in a home run by fanatical Christians. Teenage years spent without a radio, normal teenage outings, severely restricted communications (including with family), limited education, and suffocating insane religious indoctrination. The girls resembled the polygamy sect teenagers rounded up at a Texas ranch years ago (we all sported long hair and long dresses). I, too, eventually ended up in the 'furnace room' where I was confined for five weeks. The furnace room was designed to isolate you from the community and break you. If you ended up in the furnace room, it was a good bet that you were deemed demonically possessed. Yes, there was the occasional exorcism at this program. When I first arrived there, it was painful for me to intellectually forfeit what

I had learned and perceived to be truth and reason. I grasped early on that my life would be immeasurably better if I accepted their way of life. The toughest nut to crack eventually would conclude: "if you can't beat 'em, join 'em." I worked my way up to junior staff member and yes, my life was immeasurably better. However, this new persona did not jive well with the intellectual (reasoning) side of me and I could not sustain the conversion forever. After almost two and a half years of hellish incarceration, I ended up even more incarcerated after 'straying from the program': the furnace room. Midway through the five weeks, I could take no more and decided on a daring escape. I would run like crazy up the basement stairs and out the kitchen door. I tried to escape and barely made it out the kitchen door before I was subdued and physically carried back down to 'the dungeon." That was the first time in my life that I felt 'madness' and complete and utter powerlessness. Back in the 'hole', I decided on a newer, more thought out strategy. I figured the only way out, was to go along with the 'program', get re-'saved' and gradually win over their trust The ploy eventually worked and I was released back into the main house upstairs (those five isolated weeks were so, so painful, scary and lonely). Once back upstairs, I immediately began searching for an escape route. The house was always under lock-down and heavily surveyed by staff 'eyes.' By extreme good fortune and good timing, I was able to slip out the front door in a rare unguarded moment.

I knew I would have to hop the front porch and run faster than I ever ran in my entire life, which of course, I did. I ran until every breath I took felt like daggers stabbing my lungs. I had taken a few small-boxed mementos with me and they fell to the ground as I ran frantically. I desperately wanted to pick up those belongings as they were all I had of my childhood, but I knew I could not stop and risk being captured (had I been caught it could be years before I would get another chance to escape). When I felt I had run enough, I blurted out to a young bystander my story and he led me to his family home where I could use their phone to call my father. The relief I felt was palpable and my mood euphoric (what a glorious night it was to be normal again!). What I quickly learned in the following week was that I was legally free to leave but the director had convinced me I was there by court order until age 21 and that she had complete control over me! All those years wasted!! My experience at this program has a profound effect on me. After I escaped and finally emancipated, I changed my name (first, middle and last), converted to Judaism and went on to graduate summa cum laude from college. I became a psychiatric nursing administrator and got on with my life. Even so, I had nightmares for full decade after leaving (all with the same theme of being caught while escaping). To this day, I eschew religious fundamentalism of all kind. I have rarely spoken of my experiences at this program and the 34–35 years since I escaped. I came across this web site and knew

I had to share, especially since so many others had similar experiences.

Kay
United States

A man who's cancer-stricken wife died, he donated all her personal belongings to us. They were then stored under the staircase, near Mindy, unbeknown to any one, there were strong narcotics in this lot. Mindy got a hold of these drugs, and overdosed. Instead of taking someone's precious child to the ER., as they should have done, they called poison control, per instruction. To keep Mindy awake, they walked and cold showered her until they literally dragged her up and down the hall. When she could no longer walk, they laid her lifeless body on the floor. I can still see her laying there. Of course they had to call 911 then. Should they have had a way to dispose of her, I think they would have. The other thing my days off were Mondays around 8:00 or 9:00 a.m. Before I left that day, they already had knowledge she had taken these med's. She was alive and well, alert. I came back many hours later and you could tell she had got worse. This was so unnecessary. Mindy was not like her family. They were like the Cleavers, but then again, maybe she was just like her family, and was in the wrong treatment center. Her problem could not be fixed at church, I think she should have been in a hospital.

Adrienne
Indianapolis, Indiana

>Those same two directors had now opened up the 3rd phase. I was in their program for 13 ½ months. I went there pregnant towards the beginning of 08. I left there towards the end of May 09. My daughter was 1 when I left, and never did any of this info come up about what happened until now. While being there we would wait on the director hand and foot. She would spend twenty four hours a day up in her room, where we were to wait on her every need. The girls in the program were expected to eat what was cooked, and the director would call down her order, and expect it hot and made exactly the way she liked it, or none of us would eat until her food was right. I saw that director probably ten times in the whole thirteen months I was there. She would not come downstairs out of her room, unless it was for appointments. The co-director had to run the show herself. Everything she did she had to consult with the director about and the director barely knew us at all! I had my baby there and kept her there from the time she was born till she was 1, which I regret that I had to subject her to such a place. We were expected to work from 8:30 to midnight, then before bed we had night devotions, which sometimes we didn't get to bed till 2 in the morning, but were always told to be downstairs at 8:30. When my daughter started crawling, still they wanted me

working all the time. If I was in the playroom with her, the co-director would say some smart remark, "shouldn't you be working"? I would take my daughter outside because she wanted to explore. She was only a baby and the co-director would say "don't you have anything better you could be doing"? The director wanted to talk to me before I left and mind you I barely knew the lady and I went up in her office with my daughter in my lap and I will never forget what she said to me looking at my daughter "I'm so sorry pumpkin' the terrible life your mom is going to give you". I was speechless, that director is horrible, heartless, and greedy. God knows the truth about her. The man named Chris that was there in the men's home said that in her room there are empty wine bottles everywhere all kinds of empty prescription bottles, of all kinds of narcotics, just spread everywhere. It was sickening how she expected everyone to call her "mom". It wasn't a choice, it was a demand. Even the co-director and the staff did it. No one wanted to call her mom". They did it because they had to or they had nowhere else to go. My daughter was starting to walk and they expected me to work constantly and keep her in a playpen in this huge home where people walked free all over the place and anyone could grab her. I was yelled at if I was in the room with her, "being lazy", or if I wasn't in the room with her, "I was a terrible mom". The whole place is about money. Our day consisted of about an hour a day of God, six hours of sleep if lucky and seventeen hours of work. It was so ridiculous. We were making her rich on earth and definitely not in heaven, because Miss Director, you will reap what you sow and just like you said "I don't have to take account of everything you do because God does!"

Special Thanks

To Cindy Barksdale:

From the first time I walked through the doors of recovery to that first night in our small group, I will never forget how much you loved on me and truly made me feel as if someone finally truly cared. Thank you for all the time you spent with me, all the encouragement you gave me, and, more than anything, holding my hand throughout this journey and guiding me in the way I needed to go. I really don't think you understand what a huge piece you were in this puzzle and my trying to figure it out.

I remember when I first started at recovery, and on into my recovery process, while I was still hanging out at bars, it was your tears and your voice I would hear and see every time. I remember sitting at that bar, daylight coming up, and looking out the window, with your voice and the things you had told me now for over a year ringing in my head. I hung on to that at some of the worse times of my journey.

I remember sitting at your house on the couch, and sometimes you would just cry and hurt for me because I could not see what Jesus saw in me. I know you did, and you would always continue to help me to try and see myself as he did, but I just couldn't. I could never thank you enough for all the part you have played in this story. You were another one of those walking examples of Christ to me, and I am so glad God put you in my life at the time I needed you most. Thank you for walking with me as my sponsor through my first step study. I always knew I was truly blessed to have you walking that process with me. You were just a true light in my very dark world. Okay, quit crying already—again. I love you so much, and thank you, sweet friend.

To Pastor Matthew Roskam and his wife, Tammy and to all the members at Chelsea Creek Community Church:

Thank you for being such a light, strength and stability, and for walking alongside me in every step of my journey. You and Tammy were the first two people to ever believe in me and take a chance on me, even in starting my singles ministry. In doing so, you showed me what a real relationship with Jesus should look like and your example has been impeccable. You showed me what living a Christ-like life should look like by not hitting me over the head with a Bible, by not judging me, and by not making me feel as if I had to be good all the time in order for God to love me or use me. You showed me that even as broken as I was, and still am, that he could use me right at the place where I am.

You really have loved me well; you have gone way beyond the call of duty as a pastor and as a friend in all of my situations. Especially walking through the journey with my husband, you were there from the beginning to the end, supporting and encouraging him and me both, each step of the way. You continued to be my rock, my stability, and you were always there whenever I needed you, and I will never take that for granted. I greatly appreciate you both. Since trust was such a huge issue with me because of my past, you gently, over time, gained my trust and showed me I could believe and trust in other people again. My prayer is that I will be the example to others in my walk with the Lord that you and Tammy and your family have been to me. I hope to make you proud by sharing my heart through my book, with being totally vulnerable. I pray that it will bring so much hope to others, allowing me to love them well, and show others who Jesus really is. To show others who they are in Him, and who He is in them. I want to be a walking example of what Jesus can and will do in someone's life just as impeccably as you both did in mine. I love you and your whole family, and thank you.

To Art and Carie Wimberly:

I am not sure the two of you realize just how much of an impact you have both had in my life. The first time I came to recovery, it was the two of you who were serving as ministry leaders. That first night, the way the two of you ministered to me was unbelievable, and I was not expecting that from "church people". You treated me as if I mattered, and that was huge for me because it was at that exact moment in my life that I needed to know I mattered to someone. My experience that evening is what truly kept me going. I got through that night, then the next day, then another day, then another day. And yes, it was like that for a long time—one day at a time. Carie, I will never forget how loving and caring you were in the small group you were leading that night. That was the first place I knew I could be myself and not pretend anymore. It was when I saw you and heard you being so open and honest about your problems and your struggles that I remember thinking, "wow". I will never forget how after share group you two loved me, talked to me, called me in the weeks to come, and even got me to start helping with different things at recovery. I was so honored to find people who cared and loved me so much right where I was, even though I was a total mess. Art, you and Carie did a great job encouraging me to this day and have loved me in every step of my journey. Art, years later when I got married, you stepped up to the plate to help in my husband's recovery. You were amazing as his sponsor, and I know he loved you so much. The help and grace you extended to him in all he was going through was way over the call of duty as a sponsor. I knew you were struggling so bad with your depression at the time, but you so unselfishly chose to reach out and help my husband in the worst time of his life. I will also never forget, Art, you and Missy were the first two people I saw when I walked out of that room at the hospital when I was just told that my husband had shot himself and had died. I will never forget the strength you were to me during that time, and I will never take what you did for granted. I will be forever grateful to both you and Carie, and just want you to know I love you both very much.

To all my friends in Alabama's Circle of Friends:

It has been an honor and such a blessing having served as your ministry leader throughout the years. You all have pulled me through some of the worst times of my life, and I love each and every one of you. Thank you all for your tremendous support over the last seven years. I hope you realize it was every one of you that made this book even possible. Being able to walk and share life with you over the years has been truly amazing. I don't know what I would have done had I not had this circle of friends to look forward to every Saturday night. I will never forget what all of you did for me when my husband died. Each one of you took turns spending the night with me and bringing food night after night for a solid month. I don't take that lightly nor for granted. There are no words to ever say thank you. I am just so proud and so thankful that it was me that God entrusted to have served as your ministry leader. You are the most amazing circle of friends I have ever had in my life, and I love every single one of you!

To Kelley Laird and her family:

Kelley, when my husband killed himself, you so graciously opened your beautiful oasis of home to me. You let me move in with you when I had nowhere else to go. Your whole family has taken me in and treated me as if I was one of their own. I do not take that lightly or for granted. I hope you know you were a huge part of me finishing my book and my story. I would sit and look out at the beautiful view I had from my bedroom, and that is where the ending of my book was written. I am so grateful to you for extending God's grace to me in my time of need and loving me well the whole time I have been with you. I love you all.

To all my Facebook friends:

Thank you for encouraging me every day. Each one of you with keep me going by all your positive comments, likes and prayers every day. Especially when I lost my husband, all of you *really loved me through this crisis. All of your postings—and there were hundreds of them—were so overwhelming, and your concern for me was amazing. I felt so much love from all of you, although some of you I have never even met. I want you to know I am forever grateful to all of you. You know, sometimes you have nagging thoughts like wondering at times, "What do I do all this for? Are people really getting anything out of what I am doing?" The day I lost my husband was when I realized that posting the encouraging devotions every day was making a huge difference in others' lives. I knew then that pouring myself into others was exactly what God wanted me to continue to do, which, in return, took my mind off me and my problems. So thank you again for your continuing encouragement and for believing in me.*

To book Christie to come and speak to your organization 205-960-4245

Email hopeknowsyourname@gmail.com
Website: www.hopeknowsyourname.com